Foreword

This book, written by experts from eight nations, explains why imparting specific shared knowledge in early grades is important for achieving high levels of citizen competence and high levels of equality and equity. As the result of a worldwide collaboration, it is an open-access book. It is free to everyone everywhere. Special thanks is owed to Prof. Paul Kirschner of the Netherlands for herding into a unity these far-flung distinguished scholars, scientists, and public servants. Thank you, Paul!

This international effort may come to be seen in the future as the sign of a new beginning for teaching young pupils—a farewell to individualistic "child-centered" doctrines, and a ringing in of a new, more effective early education in modern democracies. The science presented in the book is up to date, some of it very recent.

Its general principles go back several years. These had their most memorable expression in a 1994 resolution approved unanimously by the Parliament of Norway—translated into English as follows by Prof. Gudmund Hernes:

> It is a tenet of popular enlightenment [i.e., the enlightenment of a whole people] that shared frames of reference must be the common property of all the people—indeed must be an integral part of general education—to escape avoidable differences in competence that can result in social inequality and be abused by undemocratic forces.
>
> Those who do not share the background information taken for granted in public discourse will often overlook the point or miss the meaning. Newcomers to a country who are not immersed in its frames of reference often remain outsiders because others cannot take for granted what they know and can do; they are in constant need of extra explanations.
>
> Common background knowledge is thus at the core of a national network of communication between members of a democratic community. It makes it possible to fathom complex messages, and to interpret new ideas, situations, and challenges. Education plays a leading role in passing on this common background information—the culture everybody must be familiar with if society is to remain democratic and its citizens sovereign.

I have not found a better summary of what this present collaborative effort has documented with the latest experimental results.

A foreword is not the place to develop a full-throated attack on the individualistic "child-centered" approach of recent decades and its incorrect empirical assumptions.

Such a polemical tone is far from the straightforward expositions of the distinguished writers from diverse lands who have produced this welcome gift. These scholars and scientists are neither accusatory nor polemical.

They show from diverse angles and fields of research that the shared knowledge revival in early grades is wrongly conceived as politically conservative. Rather, the shared knowledge approach is an essential path to equity in a democracy. These scholars from multiple nations show in detail with the latest scientific findings why a carefully sequenced shared-knowledge curriculum in early grades is essential to fairness and essential also to the complex cognitive skills demanded by modernity.

I'm grateful for the kind mentions of my own work in this book and for the invitation to write this foreword. My years in the vineyard prompt me to add this observation to the reader of this book: when the term "knowledge" is used in describing the decisive experimental results cited in this book, it will be helpful for readers to think "shared knowledge," to grasp that knowledge possession and knowledge use often involves a language transaction demanding *silently shared background knowledge between writer and reader, teacher and pupil.* Language is the means by which we humans co-ordinate our shared knowledge to create nations and achieve common goals.

That's why the word "shared" is important to connect with the word "knowledge." Knowledge gets fixed in our minds and communicated to others across generations through *shared language*, which itself depends upon shared knowledge—even when that knowledge is unstated. Human tribes flourished over other creatures in evolutionary time (as evolutionary psychologists have explained) because shared knowledge enables shared language which enables a human tribe to transform itself into a massive creature that can defeat and eat large creatures. Here's a memorable passage from the evolutionary psychologist Joseph Henrich:

> The disappearance of many megafaunal species eerily coincides with the arrival of humans on different continents and large islands. For example, before we showed up in Australia around 60,000 years ago, the continent was home to a menagerie of large animals, including two-ton wombats, immense meat-eating lizards, and leopard-sized marsupial lions. These, along with 55 other megafaunal species, went extinct in the wake of our arrival, resulting in the loss of 88% of Australia's big vertebrates.

It seems heartless to recount such a story until we consider that these lizards and marsupial lions did not achieve their immensity by picking berries. Our tribal festivals would have saved countless smaller creatures from the fearsome predators. From the viewpoint of the human tribe, the cooperative principle based upon language and shared knowledge was achieved by schooling the tribe's children.

The tribal human school was fostered by shared language built up not only for wombat-hunting techniques but also for other elements of cumulative tribal knowledge through the agency of language. A distinguished evolutionary psychologist, Michael Tomasello puts the case this way:

> Cumulative cultural evolution takes place when the inventions in a cultural group are passed on to the young with such fidelity that they remain stable in the group until a new and improved invention comes along (the so-called ratchet effect). Modern humans had a stronger ratchet

SpringerBriefs in Education

We are delighted to announce SpringerBriefs in Education, an innovative product type that combines elements of both journals and books. Briefs present concise summaries of cutting-edge research and practical applications in education. Featuring compact volumes of 50 to 125 pages, the SpringerBriefs in Education allow authors to present their ideas and readers to absorb them with a minimal time investment. Briefs are published as part of Springer's eBook Collection. In addition, Briefs are available for individual print and electronic purchase.

SpringerBriefs in Education cover a broad range of educational fields such as: Science Education, Higher Education, Educational Psychology, Assessment & Evaluation, Language Education, Mathematics Education, Educational Technology, Medical Education and Educational Policy.

SpringerBriefs typically offer an outlet for:

- An introduction to a (sub)field in education summarizing and giving an overview of theories, issues, core concepts and/or key literature in a particular field
- A timely report of state-of-the art analytical techniques and instruments in the field of educational research
- A presentation of core educational concepts
- An overview of a testing and evaluation method
- A snapshot of a hot or emerging topic or policy change
- An in-depth case study
- A literature review
- A report/review study of a survey
- An elaborated thesis

Both solicited and unsolicited manuscripts are considered for publication in the SpringerBriefs in Education series. Potential authors are warmly invited to complete and submit the Briefs Author Proposal form. All projects will be submitted to editorial review by editorial advisors.

SpringerBriefs are characterized by expedited production schedules with the aim for publication 8 to 12 weeks after acceptance and fast, global electronic dissemination through our online platform SpringerLink. The standard concise author contracts guarantee that:

- an individual ISBN is assigned to each manuscript
- each manuscript is copyrighted in the name of the author
- the author retains the right to post the pre-publication version on his/her website or that of his/her institution

Tim Surma · Claudio Vanhees · Michiel Wils ·
Jasper Nijlunsing · Nuno Crato · John Hattie ·
Daniel Muijs · Elizabeth Rata · Dylan Wiliam ·
Paul A. Kirschner

Developing Curriculum for Deep Thinking

The Knowledge Revival

 Springer

Authors
See next page

ISSN 2211-1921   ISSN 2211-193X (electronic)
SpringerBriefs in Education
ISBN 978-3-031-74660-4   ISBN 978-3-031-74661-1 (eBook)
https://doi.org/10.1007/978-3-031-74661-1

This work was supported by Thomas More Mechelen-Antwerpen vzw.

This Springer imprint is published by the registered company Springer Nature Switzerland AG
The registered company address is: Gewerbestrasse 11, 6330 Cham, Switzerland

Tim Surma
Thomas More University of Applied
Sciences
Antwerp, Belgium

Michiel Wils
Thomas More University of Applied
Sciences
Antwerp, Belgium

Nuno Crato
University of Lisboa
Lisbon, Portugal

Daniel Muijs
Queen's University Belfast
Belfast, UK

Dylan Wiliam
UCL Institute of Education
University College London
London, UK

Claudio Vanhees
Thomas More University of Applied
Sciences
Antwerp, Belgium

Jasper Nijlunsing
Thomas More University of Applied
Sciences
Antwerp, Belgium

John Hattie
The University of Melbourne
Parkville, VIC, Australia

Elizabeth Rata
The University of Auckland
Grafton, New Zealand

Paul A. Kirschner
Open University of the Netherlands
Heerlen, The Netherlands

Thomas More University of Applied
Sciences
Antwerp, Belgium

than early humans and apes because they had—in addition to powerful skills of imitation—proclivities both to teach things to others and also to conform to others when they themselves were being taught. And so it is, with this wave of group-mindedness and conformity, that we get the possibility of cultural groups creating and constantly improving their own cognitive artifacts—from procedures for whale hunting to procedures for solving differential equations.

(M. Tomasello. *A Natural History of Human Thinking*, 2014)

That *shared* knowledge principle holds true in human schooling from the primordial cave to the early American "Common School" to the jazziest use of AI in the current classroom. Shared knowledge remains the foundation of human education. So, heartfelt thanks to the distinguished authors of this open educational resource, and especially to Paul Kirschner for selflessly bringing this book into being.

Charlottesville, USA   Prof. Dr. E. D. Hirsch

Acknowledgements

We thank Daniel Willingham, Dirk Van Damme, and Henk Byls for their feedback on earlier versions of the manuscript.

Contents

Chapter 1
Introduction

Nearly all teachers and other stakeholders in education pursue a common aim: We want the students whom we teach and guide during their formative years to think deeply about what we teach them. We want them to be able to go beyond their current experiences and have a deep understanding of the world. We want to enable them to thrive and find their path through life, long after their formal education ceases. We want them to be able to think critically, work together, solve problems, read for understanding, and perform many other complex tasks. If we want students to be able to do all this, we should just include it in the curriculum and teach them, right? In this book, we discuss why this *apparently* obvious strategy of *simply teaching* children how to "think deeply" does not work, and we offer an alternative way forward.

In recent decades, many trends in the curriculum have been observed, sometimes collectively described as a *curriculum turn*. One of the characteristics of this turn is the frantic push to encourage skill acquisition with a focus on generic skills and competencies such as problem-solving, reading comprehension, collaboration, communication with each other, and so forth (Priestley & Biesta, 2013). Critics have argued that these trends have downplayed the importance of knowledge in the new curriculum (Rata, 2012; Wheelahan, 2010; Young, 2007) to the point of seeing it as either irrelevant or something that can be learned through the act of practicing these generic skills and competencies. To an extent, these criticisms have been supported by empirical evidence that shows a reduction in the specificity of content in curricula (and thus the acquisition of domain-specific knowledge) and a diminishing emphasis on the importance of knowledge in relation to general skills and competencies (Priestley & Sinnema, 2014).

The continuing decline in reading comprehension scores, as well as in science and, more recently, mathematics across several OECD countries (OECD, 2023), has highlighted the need for a renewed focus on knowledge as a necessary foundation for teaching and acquiring complex cognitive skills. Additionally, a notable shift has been observed in the OECD discourse, in which the importance of disciplinary or subject-specific knowledge is now seen as a crucial fundamental basis for equitable

© The Author(s) 2025
T. Surma et al., *Developing Curriculum for Deep Thinking*,
SpringerBriefs in Education, https://doi.org/10.1007/978-3-031-74661-1_1

opportunities (OECD, 2019). This deviates greatly from previous OECD reports that prioritised generic skills and competencies (Hughson & Wood, 2022). Social realists (Barrett, 2024), sociological theorists who have emerged as successors of constructivist thinkers (Rata, 2024a), and several cognitive psychologists now agree that a curriculum rich in domain-specific knowledge is crucial if we hope to achieve equitable opportunities for all. In line with the ideas of E. D. Hirsch (2016), they believe that focusing on rich and broad content knowledge ensures that all students, regardless of background, have equal access to a foundational body of knowledge, which helps mitigating disparities and promotes a more inclusive educational experience.

This book discusses the prominent role of knowledge in how we learn, think, read, understand, and solve problems. We draw ideas from cognitive psychology, educational psychology, sociology, and curriculum studies, and combine these ideas with case studies describing real-life classroom experiences. The publication seamlessly aligns with a clearly observable global knowledge revival: various educational systems are re-evaluating the role of knowledge in their curricula, and in a growing number of academic and non-academic publications the role of knowledge to promote equity, unity and progress in a modern society is emphasised. Our goal is therefore to explain why a knowledge-rich curriculum is the soundest way forward to both effectively teach knowledge and complex skills in school.

References

Barrett, B. (2024). Rob Moore, social realism, and the sociology of education and knowledge. In E. Rata (Ed.), *Research handbook in curriculum and education*, Chap. 5 (pp. 79–87) Edward Elgar Publishing.

Hirsch, E. D. (2016). *Why knowledge matters: Rescuing our children from failed educational theories*. Harvard Education Press.

Hughson, T. A., & Wood, B. E. (2022). The OECD Learning Compass 2030 and the future of disciplinary learning: A Bernsteinian critique. *Journal of Education Policy, 37*(4), 634–654.

OECD. (2019). Conceptual learning framework: Knowledge for 2030 concept note. https://www.oecd.org/education/2030-project/teaching-and-learning/learning/knowledge/in_brief_Knowledge.pdf

OECD. (2023). PISA 2022 Results (Volume I): The state of learning and equity in education, PISA, OECD Publishing.

Priestley, M., & Biesta, G. (Eds.). (2013). *Reinventing the curriculum: New trends in curriculum policy and practice*. A&C Black.

Priestley, M., & Sinnema, C. (2014). Downgraded curriculum? An analysis of knowledge in new curricula in Scotland and New Zealand. In *Creating curricula: Aims, knowledge and control* (pp. 61–86). Routledge.

Rata, E. (2012). The politics of knowledge in education. *British Educational Research Journal, 38*, 103–124.

Rata, E. (2024). Introduction: Social realism, didaktik, and cognitive science in curriculum and education. In E. Rata (Ed.), *Research handbook on curriculum and education* (pp. 1–18). Edward Elgar Publishing.

Wheelahan, L. (2010). *Why knowledge matters in curriculum: A social realist argument*. Routledge.

Young, M. (2007). *Bringing knowledge back in: From social constructivism to social realism in the sociology of education*. Routledge.

Chapter 2
How Knowledge Matters

Abstract We, in education, all have a common aim: We want students to be able to think deeply about what we teach them, go beyond their current experiences, and have a deep understanding of the world. We want to enable them to think critically, work together, solve problems, read for understanding, and carry out complex cognitive tasks. If we want students to be able to do all this, we should just include itt in the curriculum and teach them, right? In this chapter, we discuss why this *apparently* obvious strategy of *simply teaching* children how to think deeply does not work, and offer an alternative way forward. This chapter discusses the prominent role of knowledge in how we learn, think, read, understand, and solve problems. Insights from cognitive and educational psychology, sociology, and curriculum studies are used to underpin the current knowledge revival that is widely being observed in education.

Keywords Knowledge-rich · Education · Knowledge acquisition · Complex cognitive skills · Democratic citizenship

> "What we know is a drop
> what we don't know is an ocean" (Isaac Newton).

What you know determines what you see (Kirschner, 1991). Another and possibly more prosaic way of saying this is: Knowledge begets knowing. The more extensive one's knowledge-base is in terms of both its breadth and its depth the more easily new knowledge is acquired and remembered (Alexander et al., 1994; Ausubel, 1968; Shapiro, 2004). Knowledge is also essential for carrying out the complex cognitive skills such as critical thinking (you think critically about something) problem-solving (you solve problems in something) and reading comprehension (you comprehend something written about something). The more robust one's knowledge-base the more seamlessly and efficiently these complex cognitive skills—which require students to "think deeply" and are precisely those that teachers aim to develop in their students—are acquired and can be carried out. The subsequent chapter describes the significance of knowledge from cognitive sociological and democratic perspectives. These different perspectives draw on various research traditions each with its own procedures and standards for what constitutes a convincing argument. What is presented is therefore a mixture of scientific and humanities approaches all serving the objective of illustrating the critical role of knowledge in promoting deep thinking.

2.1 Knowledge Matters: A Learning Perspective

2.1.1 A Basic Understanding of Human Cognitive Architecture

We need to examine our cognitive architecture to understand where knowledge fits within human cognition. Some forms of knowledge appear to be acquired effortlessly due to our evolutionary development over numerous millennia. Such knowledge, resulting in skills like communicating with those around us, speaking our mother tongue, recognising facial expressions and physical signals, recognising others, understanding the relation between an incline and things rolling down from it … is recognised by evolutionary psychologists as being biologically (or evolutionarily) primary knowledge (Geary & Berch, 2016). In contrast, a second category consists of knowledge that is more recent in nature. It was not until a couple of hundred or even thousand years ago that most people in a few societies learned to read and write, solve algebraic problems, and engage in discussions about geographical, scientific, political, cultural, and historical phenomena. This category of knowledge is known as biologically (or evolutionarily) secondary knowledge and, unlike our innate ability to seemingly effortlessly acquire the first category (without many/most of them a person could not live long enough to procreate), we lack a natural mechanism to just as effortlessly assimilate the second—more cultural—category through mere exposure. It must be consciously taught and effortfully learned, building upon, yet distinct from biologically primary knowledge. Schools were established to impart this biologically secondary knowledge that is rarely acquired spontaneously, as it is vital for functioning in contemporary societies. When we speak of knowledge in educational systems, we mainly refer to biologically secondary knowledge, and cognitive psychologists have been investigating how human cognitive architecture processes this information for many decades.

Broadbent (1958) is considered one of the first scientists to use an information processing metaphor to portray the human attentional processing system. He postulated, around the same time as Miller (1957; The Magical Number Seven, Plus or Minus Two), that humans have a limited capacity to process information and, due to this limited capacity, a selective filter—acting like a bottleneck—is needed for information processing. He compared human information processing capacity to a limited amount of information that can be conveyed through a given channel at a given time: "if we send a Morse code with a buzzer, we cannot send a dot and a dash at the same time, but must send them successively" (Broadbent, 1958, p. 5).

Shortly thereafter, Atkinson and Shiffrin (1968) put forward a multi-store model of memory composed of *a sensory memory* where information from all of our senses enters memory; *a short-term memory* (STM) which receives and retains input from both the sensory memory and the long-term store; and finally this *long-term store*, where information that has been repeatedly rehearsed in the short-term store is permanently stored.

Subsequently, Baddeley and Hitch (1974) proposed a new memory model that challenged the prevailing view of short-term memory. They suggested that short-term memory is composed of multiple, distinct components that work together, allowing us to hold information in our minds and manipulate it. This is what became known as *working memory* (WM). In their original work, they spoke of a verbal and visual store, but more recent research (e.g., Baddeley & Andrade, 2000) has expanded this to include other memory stores such as olfactory, gustatory, and tactile. Baddeley and Hitch also discussed the role of long-term memory in working memory, noting that it plays a crucial role in the ability to hold and manipulate information over longer periods of time. They suggested that working memory and long-term memory are separate but interdependent systems. This led to a widely used and functionally practical memory model, which is simplified in Fig. 2.1 (based on Willingham, 2021).

Working memory is essentially the cognitive workspace in which information is temporarily stored and acted upon. That is, it is the system that supports our capacity to "keep things in mind" when carrying out complex tasks. For instance, when pondering the question: "What similarities exist between a raincoat and a notebook?" we would extract pertinent details about raincoats (e.g., water-resistant, worn outdoors, protective gear) and notebooks (e.g., bound pages, used for writing, portable) from long-term memory. The next step would involve assessing these characteristics for any commonalities (Willingham, 2019). We carry this out in our working memory. Working memory capacity is notably finite, having a capacity for only four to seven unconnected elements at any given time. We cannot hold a lot in

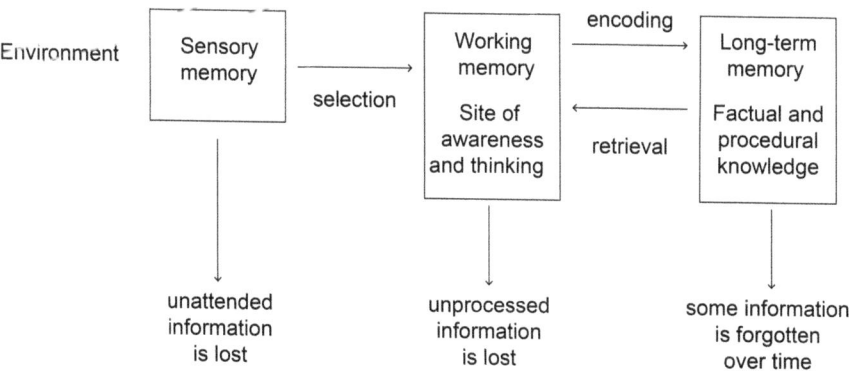

Fig. 2.1 A simple representation of human memory (based on Willingham, 2021)

our working memory, and even the small amount we can hold does not remain there for a very long time (i.e., 3–20 s) if nothing is done with it. Imagine being asked to identify a common attribute among a raincoat, a notebook, a teaspoon, a guitar, and a refrigerator. Our working memory could possibly retain the names of these five items, but supporting details for each item and the cognitive resources to evaluate them collectively would exceed our processing limitations.

Let's look at a second example that illustrates the constraints of working memory. Imagine you have to learn the chemical interactions below:

$$2\,NaCN + H_2O + CO_2 = Na_2CO_3 + 2HCN$$
$$2H + CNO_2CNa_2O : NaH_3 + 2CCN_2O$$

You are exposed to these formulas for 30 s each. After one minute, they are hidden, and you are asked to write them down. How well did you do? Well, it probably depends. This experiment, a modern-day version of de Groot (1965) studies with chess masters, was conducted with experts and non-experts in chemistry (Zhilin & Tkachuk, 2013). After respondents in both groups were exposed to the equations for 30 s, experts immediately recognised that the first equation represented a reaction in which sodium cyanide ($NaCN$) reacts with water (H_2O) and carbon dioxide (CO_2) to produce sodium carbonate (Na_2CO_3) and hydrogen cyanide (HCN). The experts also recalled real chemical equations better than the novice participants, but experts and novices had no significant difference in recalling the fake equation. Novices tended to remember both real and fake equations symbol-by-symbol from left to right, with increasing mistakes in the same order. On the other hand, experts remembered the real equation as a whole, and could chunk (combine smaller, unitary bits of information into larger and more meaningful ones) some chains in the fake sequences, resulting in slightly better memory.

These findings support the idea that experts can *chunk* information based on the knowledge in their long-term memory and can see patterns in new situations. They combine (or "chunk") smaller bits of knowledge into a single knowledge unit. This chunking (combining smaller units of information into larger ones) is a function of our prior knowledge in our long-term memory. Long-term memory, thus, assists working memory while thinking. It is an expansive repository within our cognitive structure that possesses a seemingly limitless capacity for storing information. It facilitates the consolidation of discrete elements into coherent wholes (i.e., chunks), thereby economising scarce working memory resources. The first chemical equation probably only contains one chunk of information for the expert. This frees cognitive space from working memory—a cognitive shortcut—to consider other aspects of the task. It makes learning look easier as the information needed to carry out the task pops up seemingly effortless. What you already know does not require much mental effort, so experts with vast amounts of domain-specific knowledge can tackle new problems in their domain of expertise more efficiently (i.e., with more speed and accuracy) than novices do (Willingham, 2021). The key words here are 'in their domain'. A good chess player is not a good checkers or go-player, just as the chemists in the experiment cannot do this when dealing with a geology problem let alone a problem dealing with a language they do not speak. Their skill is not generic, but rather specific to particular subject matter—what psychologists call 'domain-specific'.

Knowledge is stored in long-term memory in cognitive structures or schemas. They can be seen as structures of organised and interconnected knowledge elements comprising concepts, words, and ideas. Schemas can also consist of other schemas, much like how the concept of 'a tree' can be explained in terms of its roots, trunk, branches, leaves, and fruits. Each of these terms can also be broken down further, such as the veins, chlorophyll, and cells of a leaf. Renn (2020) refers to these complex interdependencies as the 'architecture of knowledge'. However, schemas are not permanently fixed. We can also start from 'inside the box' and expand it in a different direction. For instance, starting from the concept of chlorophyll, one may discover examples such as green pasta or spirits, in which chlorophyll is used as a colouring additive (E140). In other words, knowledge can be organised into various hierarchies, forming complex schemas of interconnected ideas, and serve as conceptual coat hangers or anchors for the organisation of knowledge and learning new ideas (Hattie, 2023).

2.1.2 How Can Prior Knowledge Facilitate Better Learning?

Possessing knowledge and skills in long-term memory frees up valuable space in working memory to tackle more complex cognitive thinking tasks such as problem-solving, critical thinking, and reading comprehension, as discussed below. If you have ever wondered why we have elementary school students memorise the multiplication tables, drill verb conjugations, perfect their spelling, expand their vocabulary, and acquire background knowledge, the following will help you to understand. It's all about automaticity. Seemingly counterintuitively, the best ways to become proficient in a skill often do not resemble the skill itself (Wiliam, 2018). For instance, if someone wants to become proficient at playing a musical instrument like the piano, they might find that simply playing the piano for hours on end isn't the most efficient way to improve. A novice piano player might first want to train and automate certain hand movements or learn about music theory. Outside education, this subtle understanding of the importance of automaticity is well understood and is often seen as a precondition for true mastery. How many passionate young football (in America: soccer) players meticulously practice isolated dribbling techniques to succeed on the pitch? And how many actors or musicians memorise their lines or riffs to be able to improvise on stage? Beyond improving on the practiced task, this approach has the added benefit of conserving 'mental bandwidth' to do more. And it goes even further than that. Try to study the following three rows of twelve digits.

Row 1 : 610894121158

Row 2 : 106614921815

Row 3 : 198520192023

Which row do you remember best? Let's take a guess. You found row 1 to be the hardest to learn. Row 3 was the easiest to learn because you possibly saw it as referring to recent years. Row 2 could also be easy to remember, yet only if you have sufficient background knowledge of history: 1066 was the year of the Battle of Hastings; in 1492 Columbus 'discovered' America, and in 1815 Napoleon met his Waterloo. However, if you do not possess this background knowledge, Row 2 would appear as difficult as Row 1. Knowledge in your long-term memory not only reduces the complexity and difficulty of acquiring new knowledge (i.e., turning added information into knowledge), it also seems easier to do so, while simultaneously enhancing retention. Whereas the numbers from Row 1 might already be fading from memory, those from Rows 2 and 3 are more likely to remain embedded in memory. That is because new information that can be connected to prior knowledge tends to stick around longer. The slower you forget, the longer you retain. Psychologists have spent decades studying the processes involved in slowing down forgetting and effectively storing knowledge in long-term memory. They have identified a range of learning strategies, the detailed exploration of which lies beyond the scope of this book. For a brief introduction, see Appendix A.

If prior knowledge supports thinking, makes learning easier, and leads to more durable learning, it is tempting to conclude that our children simply need to learn a vast amount of knowledge. Right? The more prior knowledge, the better. Yet, this is the point at which we must proceed with caution. Whether and how prior knowledge influences learning depends on the nature of that prior knowledge itself (Brod, 2021). Knowledge alone does not lead to better learning. To be effective, prior knowledge must meet several important criteria.

First, it must be **activated**. For example, imagine students learning about the formation of the Himalayas. Potentially relevant prior knowledge might include understanding what a mountain range is and how plate tectonics play a role in this, knowing that the Himalayas are located in Asia at the point where two plates collide, and that Asia is a continent that includes India and most of Russia, among other facts. Some children might even have a basic understanding of concepts such as shifting tectonic plates and continental drift. The issue of prior knowledge not being activated by learners has been extensively researched, particularly in children, who often have not yet become resourceful in using cognitive control strategies to use their prior knowledge strategically. On the other hand, well integrated knowledge will become active on its own. In essence, it is not enough for prior knowledge to be available; it must also be (consciously or unconsciously) activated and applied to guide the learning process. The teacher's role is critical here, tasked with mapping out what children should already know to fully comprehend the content of a new lesson and activating it, for example, with pre-questions (retrieval practice) or advance organisers.

Second, even if learners activate some prior knowledge, it must also be **relevant** to the learning task to be beneficial. Students might know about India's extensive colonial history with Britain and that the British set up hill stations in the foothills of the Himalayas, but this information is not really helpful when trying to understand geological formations in the Himalayas. Students might even hold misconceptions (i.e., faulty beliefs) about plate tectonics, such as wrongly assuming that each continent rests on a separate tectonic plate, with continental boundaries aligning with plate edges. This could make it harder for them to grasp the role of India in the northward thrust that continues to elevate the Himalayas today. Irrelevant and faulty prior knowledge might even hinder subsequent learning (Simonsmeier et al., 2022).

Finally, prior knowledge should ideally be congruent with the new information even when activated and relevant. For instance, within the geography curriculum, certain words such as plate, drift, and mantle possess technical definitions that may prove challenging for students to comprehend because of the presence of alternative, common-sense or common-language meanings of those words that significantly deviate from their technical connotations. The greater the necessary reorganisation of existing knowledge, the more challenging it can be for learners to integrate new information into existing knowledge schemas. While higher congruency between prior knowledge and new information usually enhances learning of the new information, it has been demonstrated that highly incongruent new information can also be effectively learned, particularly when it triggers a significant level of surprise in learners (Brode, 2021). Thus, the complex nature of prior knowledge underscores that its impact on learning depends on more than simply the quantity of knowledge available. However, if prior knowledge is activated, relevant, and congruent, then its impact on learning can be significant.

2.1.3 Why Complex Cognitive Skills Require Knowledge

While knowledge storage and schema building in long term memory are important, they are not enough. We are greedy. Education should also have the ambition to engage with this knowledge and foster the acquisition and use of complex cognitive skills in students such as critical thinking, problem solving, and reading comprehension. However, the question arises as to whether critical thinking or any of these complex cognitive skills can be generically taught across or without reference to specific knowledge domains. If you ask historians to describe what critical thinking is, they say very similar things to what mathematicians say. Hence, it is natural to think that they are the same skill. In contrast, they are in fact a collection of superficially similar skills (e.g., evaluating the relevancy of certain things or determining the validity of an argument) and/or procedures (i.e., the steps to take in carrying out research) that rely on different underlying cognitive processes. While it should be acknowledged that the idea of teaching generalised critical thinking skills is attractive, we should not consider those processes as a collection of skills that can be employed at any given time or in any given context. Those who have endeavoured to teach complex skills such as critical thinking as a separate course in the curriculum have operated under the assumption that it is a skill akin to driving a car, and once acquired, can be applied in any given situation. They assumed students who learned to think critically in history lessons about, for instance, the role of the French revolution in nation-building in Europe, would transfer those critical thinking skills to novel situations, such as critical thinking about zero-emission policies to combat global warming. Or they assumed that students who learned to solve open-ended problems in physics would be able to transfer that skill to solve problems in psychology. The steps seem similar or identical, but cognitive science research has revealed that critical thinking or other complex cognitive skills are not of that nature. The processes of thought are intricately intertwined with the *content* of the thoughts themselves; in other words, with domain-specific knowledge.

In a landmark experiment, researchers presented participants with a scenario illustrating an ill-defined problem wherein an X-ray, capable of treating a tumour, also posed the risk of damaging a lot of healthy tissue:

> Suppose you are a doctor faced with a patient who has a malignant tumor in his stomach. It is impossible to operate on the patient, but unless the tumor is destroyed the patient will die. There is a kind of ray that can be used to destroy the tumor. If the rays reach the tumor all at once at a sufficiently high intensity, the tumor will be destroyed. Unfortunately, at this intensity the healthy tissue that the rays pass through on the way to the tumor will also be destroyed. At lower intensities the rays are harmless to healthy tissue, but they will not affect the tumor either. What type of procedure might be used to destroy the tumor with the rays, and at the same time avoid destroying the healthy tissue? (Gick & Holyoak, 1983, pp. 3)

Participants were thus tasked with determining how to use the X-ray to eliminate the tumour, a problem that only a minority solved within 20 min. Subsequently, another group was exposed to a military scenario mirroring this dilemma, but it was solvable in the same way. In this scenario, a general plans to seize a fortress situated at the heart of a country. The fortress is accessible by several roads, but each is heavily mined. While small groups can pass the roads safely, a large force would detonate the mines. To overcome this, the general splits his army into smaller units, sends each along a different road, and has them converge on the fortress at the same time. The "convergence" solution to the military problem is analogous to the X-ray problem (i.e., scattering the forces to avoid collateral damage and having forces converge at the point of attack). Despite reading this story immediately prior to addressing the medical problem, they failed to perceive the analogy with the convergence solution, as depicted in Fig. 2.2. Remarkably, solution rates surged when the story was explicitly mentioned (Gick & Holyoak, 1983).

This underscores the idea that employing the analogy in a novel situation was not the main challenge; rather, the difficulty lies in recalling it and seeing its need or

Fig. 2.2 Schemes that illustrate the principle underlying the convergence solution

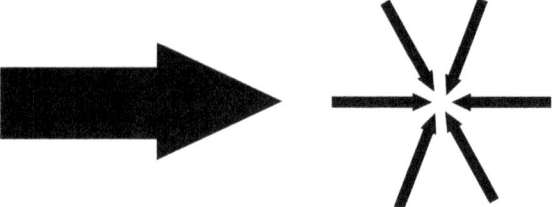

usefulness. These findings offered crucial insights into teaching critical thinking. The challenge in transferring critical thinking skills lies in the fact that domain-specific examples on how to think critically should be offered to students (they will act as worked examples for future similar tasks), and that they are archived in long-term memory, and resurface only using specific triggers.

The ability to think critically about open-ended problems such as the radiation problem described above is facilitated by vast knowledge in the specific area. Knowledge plays a role in solving these problems in at least three ways (Willingham, 2019). First, as described earlier, knowledge from long-term memory assists working memory because of the experts' ability to chunk new information into new or already existing coherent wholes. Recognising a situation similar to a previously encountered one helps you identify areas of strength and weakness, thereby freeing up valuable thinking space in working memory. Second, the recognition process of the open-ended problem ('ah, this is a radiation problem') can still be applied to components of a yet more complex, open-ended problem. Complex critical thinking may involve the application of multiple simpler solutions from memory, which can be combined when solving new, more complex problems. The final way in which knowledge can contribute to critical thinking is by enabling the individual to employ thinking strategies in combination with domain-specific knowledge, stored in long-term memory. When discussing the recognition of underlying structures such as in the radiation problem, the issue arose from having an effective thinking strategy stored in memory, yet failing to retrieve it due to a lack of recognition of its relevance for the particular situation. However, some situations that require critical thinking can be easily identified. For instance, we can teach graduate students in a certain domain to evaluate the logic behind scientists' arguments and prompt them to assess whether students can infer causal claims with the scientific methodology used. Those graduate students should have no difficulty recognising the type of problem they are facing and may have already stored the correct thinking strategy in long-term memory, in this case combined with some statistical knowledge. They know what needs to be done, yet they might still face the problem of not having the necessary domain-specific knowledge, which may hinder their ability to utilise the strategy.

Complex cognitive skills such as critical thinking are therefore not a collection of skills that can be employed at any given time or in any given context. They should be seen as a form of thought that requires knowledge with which to engage. The same applies to the other complex cognitive thinking skills to a greater or lesser extent. It would be amazing if we could teach our students to solve open-ended problems in geography in a way that would also improve their ability to solve open-ended problems in mathematics, yet this is not how our brains work. Problem-solving in geography requires students to learn specific geographical content knowledge. No matter how much we train students to solve math problems or teach them Latin, it does not make them better 'problem-solvers' or 'logical thinkers' in other domains such as in a natural science (De Bruyckere et al., 2020; Thorndike, 1923). It remains clear that without relevant prior knowledge, cross-discipline learning is not what many in education once hoped it would be. Interestingly, the PISA 2022 survey included *Creativity* as an additional domain, yet it revealed a high correlation between mathematical knowledge and creativity, indicating a strong relationship between higher-order skills and domain knowledge (OECD, 2024; Ward & Kolomyts, 2010).

However, this does not imply that problem-solving without prior knowledge is consistently ineffective. At times, it can be beneficial to start with problem-solving in a particular topic to identify what students already know and need to learn and motivate them to dig deeper. This is often the case in goal-free or goal-nonspecific problems where learners are given information (objects, their mass, angle of incline, friction) and then are asked to determine what they can do with it (Ayres, 1993; Van Merriënboer & Kirschner, 2017). Take the following example from Van Merriënboer and Kirschner (2017, p. 73):

> Usually, learners receive goal-specific problems, such as "A car with a mass of 950 kg accelerating in a straight line from rest for 10 seconds travels 100 meters. What is the final velocity of the car?" This problem could easily be made goal nonspecific by replacing the last line with 'Calculate the value of as many of the variables involved here as you can.' Here, the learner would calculate the final velocity, acceleration, and force exerted by the car at top acceleration. And if the word 'calculate' was replaced by 'represent,' the learner could also include graphs and the like. Nonspecific goal problems invite learners to move forward from the givens and to explore the problem space, which may help them construct cognitive schemas.

This can then be followed by more targeted teaching and knowledge building, and finally returning to problem-solving to reinforce their understanding (Kapur, 2008).

2.1.4 Reading Comprehension

"Reading is the basis for the acquisition of knowledge, for cultural engagement, for democracy, and for success in the workplace" (Castles et al., 2018, p. 5). Moreover, its importance in education cannot be overstated as it is essential for further learning in all subjects. At the same time, reading is one of the most complex mental acts a person can do and entails the development of cognitive thinking skills in five areas, the so called 'big five': phonics, phonemic awareness, vocabulary, fluency, and language comprehension (National Reading Panel, 2000; National Research Council, 2000; RAND Reading Study Group, 2002; Pearson & Cervetti, 2015). In the following paragraphs it will become clear to you as a skilled reader just how many complex processes are being executed in your mind while you read this book, and why this is important when teaching reading to students.

The schematic model in Fig. 2.3 (Willingham, 2017) summarises the complexity of the cognitive processes involved in reading at roughly three highly interconnected levels: (1) letters and phonemes; (2) words; and (3) sentences, paragraphs, and full texts.

When teaching reading, the most effective programs first address the development of alphabet knowledge, phonemic awareness, and oral language (i.e., listening and oral fluency), the so-called prereading skills. Most children already possess relatively developed spoken-language skills, including knowledge of the meanings

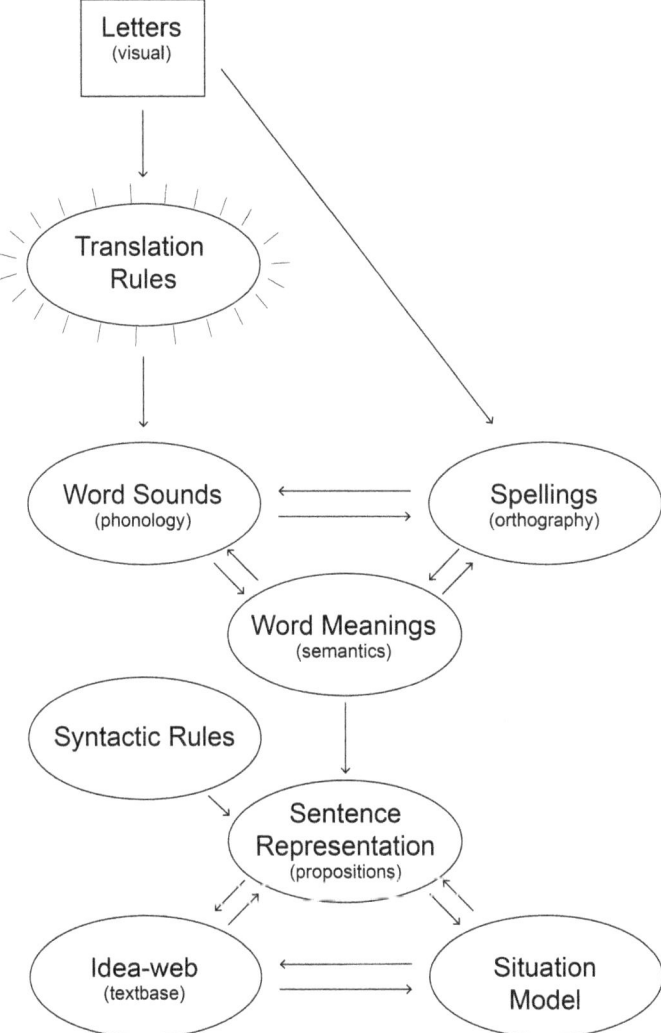

Fig. 2.3 Model of reading (Willingham, 2017)

of many spoken words, when they start to learn how to read (Castles et al., 2018). Subsequently, a focus on explicit and implicit vocabulary instruction, comprehension, and phonics instruction with repeated opportunities to read—silently and aloud—to develop fluency is considered the most powerful combination for early reading instruction (Hattie, 2023). The Reading Rope, a visual representation created by Hollis Scarborough, helps us understand the complex processes involved in how the brain learns to read (see Fig. 2.4). The two meta-strands, language comprehension and word recognition, once again contain their own subsets of distinct components.

In the case of language comprehension those are background knowledge, vocabulary, language structures, verbal reasoning and literacy knowledge, and with regard to word recognition respectively phonological awareness, decoding and sight recognition are involved. Language comprehension and word recognition are interconnected and interdependent, so when students progress toward fluency with sufficient practice and instruction, word recognition becomes increasingly automatic, and language comprehension becomes increasingly strategic (Scarborough et al., 2009).

With sufficient mastery, the initially heavy demand on students' working memories while reading is gradually reduced. This means they can commit more cognitive resources to comprehending what they are reading, that is, the complex mental processes involved in constructing meaning from and in individual sentences, across paragraphs, and finally in full texts. Principles similar to those in reading also apply

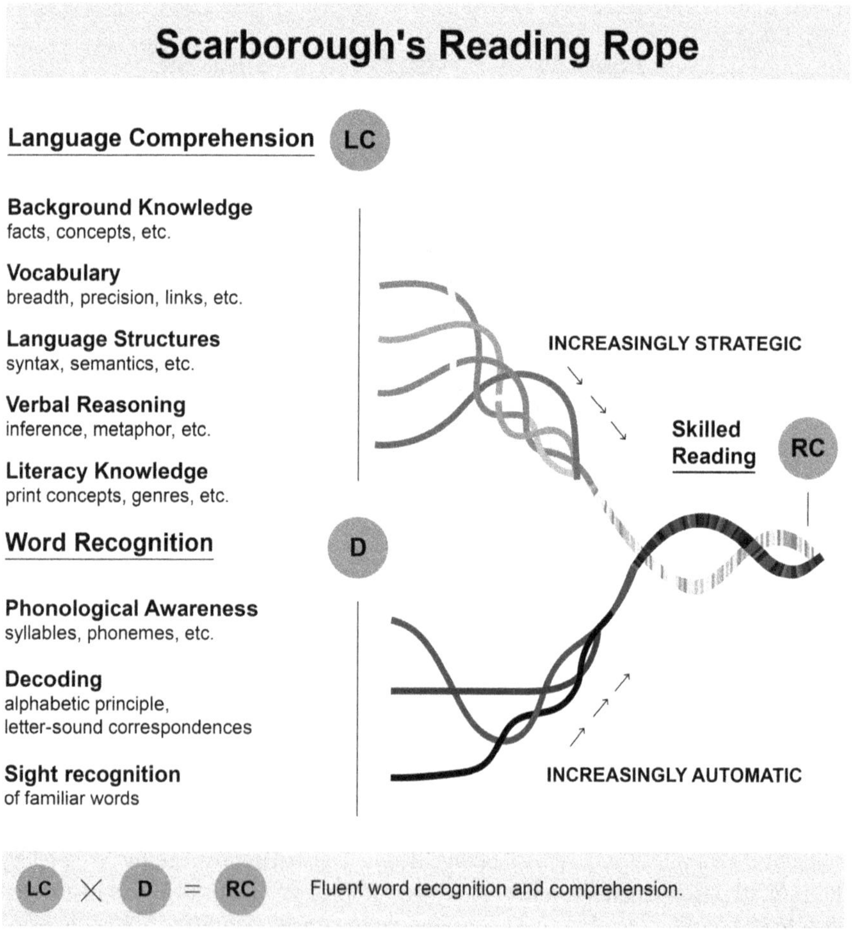

Scarborough's Reading Rope

Language Comprehension LC

Background Knowledge
facts, concepts, etc.

Vocabulary
breadth, precision, links, etc.

Language Structures
syntax, semantics, etc.

Verbal Reasoning
inference, metaphor, etc.

Literacy Knowledge
print concepts, genres, etc.

Word Recognition D

Phonological Awareness
syllables, phonemes, etc.

Decoding
alphabetic principle,
letter-sound correspondences

Sight recognition
of familiar words

INCREASINGLY STRATEGIC

Skilled
Reading RC

INCREASINGLY AUTOMATIC

LC × D = RC   Fluent word recognition and comprehension.

Fig. 2.4 Reading rope (Scarborough et al., 2009)

to arithmetic fluency and math problem solving as among others David Geary (2011), and Xin Lin and Sarah Powell (2022) have shown in their work.

In what follows, we describe how knowledge elements play a role at each of the interconnected levels as described in the overall Model of Reading depicted in Fig. 2.3, to facilitate the gradual development of those complex reading processes that distinguish successful from struggling readers, and how background knowledge plays a particularly important role in deep reading comprehension at the level of sentences, paragraphs, and full-texts.

2.1.4.1 Letters and Phonemes

Letter knowledge and phonemic awareness are the first requirements for learning how to decode text in alphabetic languages (Ehri et al., 2001; Ruan et al., 2018), namely to be able to "distinguish one letter from another, hear individual speech sounds, and know the mapping between letters (and letter groups), and speech sounds" (Willingham, 2017 p. 47). Consequently, an important component of initial reading instruction is effectively teaching letters and awareness of individual speech sounds, so that students' knowledge of the relationships between speech sounds and (groups of) letters (the alphabetic principle) can become increasingly automatised (Hattie, 2023). With sufficient practice, students can then apply it through phonics; that is, use their knowledge of the relationships between speech sounds and (groups of) letters to decode text, and read familiar and unfamiliar words.

2.1.4.2 Words

Word-specific knowledge. While initially very demanding, with extensive practice students can gradually automate the letter-sound translation process (sounding a word out), and reduce the demands on their working memories. As the comprehension processes in reading in the next phases are so demanding, it is very important that readers can free up enough space in working memory by making reading faster and easier. At the word level, this requires word-specific knowledge (Perfetti, 2007), which implies that readers need to develop very strong relationships between word sounds, spellings, and meanings (see the middle part of Willingham's model, Fig. 2.3), which in turn will provide them with nearly automatic word recognition. Extensive practice in reading individual words and later sentences and texts, as well as explicit spelling and morphology instruction (Graham & Santangelo, 2014) and explicit vocabulary instruction, can boost this process. That way, students' reading fluency is built over months and years.

Vocabulary breadth and depth. Vocabulary knowledge in the broad sense is very important, as both vocabulary breadth (i.e., knowing many words) and depth (i.e., having many and strong connections between words) matter to reading comprehension (Elleman et al., 2009; Nation & Snowling, 1998; Ouellette, 2006). Deep vocabulary knowledge not only includes knowing the meanings of words (i.e., semantics), their structure (i.e., morphology), spelling, and use (i.e., grammar), but also links to other words (i.e., word/semantic relationships).

In terms of vocabulary breadth, research has shown that readers need to know up to 95 percent of the words in a text to understand it at a general level, and even 98 percent to really comprehend it (Carver, 1994; Hsueh-Chao & Nation, 2000; Schmitt et al., 2011). If this so-called coverage drops to 80 percent, readers can at best only understand the overall gist of a text (Nation, 2001), and most readers would find it so difficult to extract the gist that they would likely give up. Sometimes, the meaning of unknown words can be derived from the context, but only to a limited extent. To do so, readers would already need to have a relatively large vocabulary, and the coverage in the specific text they read would need to be nearly 98 percent, or only one unknown word for every 50 known words (Hsueh-Chao & Nation, 2000; Laufer, 1992; Laufer & Yano, 2001). Moreover, too much task-switching between problem-solving and comprehension during reading occupies working memory resources required for understanding and can therefore interrupt the flow of reading (Csik-szentmihalyi, 1990; Kirschner & De Bruyckere, 2017; Willingham, 2017). Regular interruptions make reading less fluent, more difficult, and less enjoyable. For the same reason, looking up the meaning of unknown words in, for instance, online glossaries is only of limited use, and they have the additional disadvantage that word definitions are offered in just one context, whereas the meaning of words is precisely very sensitive to the context in which it appears (Willingham, 2017).

The importance of vocabulary depth is somewhat more difficult to understand, but we will try to illustrate it with an example. Students may know that a scorpion is an animal with a pair of grasping pincers and a long tail. If that is all they know, do they then know the word 'scorpion'? Yes, but only in a shallow way. Deeper knowledge of the word would also invoke connections to concepts like 'predatory', 'the desert', 'stinger', and 'venomous'. This is important, as different facets can be required for understanding in different contexts, and authors often omit information (i.e. background knowledge) they expect their readership to know. So if students only know that a scorpion is an animal with a pair of grasping pincers similar to a crab's that has a long tail, a precautionary message like 'Don't pick up a scorpion, and definitely watch out for its tail.' might inform them to a certain extent. However, someone who also knows that it has a venomous stinger, and uses it not only to hunt, but also to defend itself, will be much better informed before approaching a scorpion.

This example shows how words are situated in meaning networks, and how they activate related words. That depth of your vocabulary knowledge helps you fill in the 'gaps' between sentences and paragraphs, as authors implicitly expect you to possess certain background knowledge to understand the ideas conveyed in the texts they write, yet they do not explicitly include it all. That would simply render most texts extremely long and unreadable. Besides the richness of those word relationships, also the speed you can access them with facilitates reading (Oakhill et al., 2012). As mentioned above, that speed is determined by the strength of the relationships between word sounds, spellings, and meanings, also known as readers' word-specific knowledge (Perfetti, 2007).

Sentences, paragraphs, and full texts. When it comes to deep reading comprehension at the sentence, paragraph, and text level, the construction-integration (CI) model of text comprehension (Kintsch, 1998; Kintsch & van Dijk, 1978) remains the most detailed interactive model to describe the mental processes in the minds of readers (integrated in the lower part of Willingham's model; Fig. 2.3). It describes how the words and syntax are situated in a text's surface structure, from which readers later create sentence representations (also called propositions). Readers then construct a text-base model (or idea-web; Willingham, 2017) by connecting these propositions in the text's main idea. This text-base model represents quite literally 'what the text says' and is subsequently inserted in their working memories. Besides sufficiently automated basic reading processes described above at the letter, phoneme, and word level, students also need knowledge of syntactic rules and text structure to facilitate this mental construction of the main idea of the paragraph or text they read.

However, this main idea of the text alone is not enough for deep understanding. This is where background knowledge comes into play. Only through the integration of the text-base with relevant background knowledge and experiences from long-term memory (readers' pre-existing schemas) can readers truly come to a deeper understanding of a text. The mental model that is subsequently created is called the situation model (Zwaan & Radvansky, 1998), and is a reader's dynamically constructed detailed mental representation of the text. Besides readers' overall language and decoding ability as described, now the breadth and depth of their background knowledge, including vocabulary, comes into play, which differs among students, thus leading to distinct situation models for each reader. Four intersecting dimensions of background knowledge can thereby be distinguished (McCarthy & McNamara, 2021):

(1) amount (how many relevant concepts readers already know);
(2) accuracy (how correct the knowledge is that readers already possess);
(3) specificity (how related their knowledge is to the information in the text); and
(4) coherence (how interconnected the knowledge is that readers already possess).

The good news is that situation models are also cumulative; so, if the same reader becomes more knowledgeable about a topic, the schemas and situation model will evolve (Kintsch, 1998). However, if students lack the necessary background knowledge to integrate the text base, a less effective situation model results, and they consequently experience more difficulty understanding a text (Kendeou & Van Den Broek, 2007).

The previous sections have shown that "while word knowledge speeds up word recognition and thus the process of reading, world knowledge speeds up comprehension of textual meaning by offering a foundation for making inferences (Hirsch, 2003, p. 12)." Let us now more closely consider how background knowledge facilitates deep reading comprehension.

The Importance of Background Knowledge. A review study on experimental research with primary-school aged children on the role of background knowledge in reading comprehension (Smith et al., 2021) has confirmed the critical importance of both reading ability (the upper part of Willingham's model, Fig. 2.3) and background knowledge (the lower part) for deep reading comprehension. It was found that higher levels of background knowledge on a topic, both in terms of quantity and quality, consistently lead to better text comprehension in both high- and low-ability readers, and that increased background knowledge impacts reading comprehension differently in students with distinct reading ability. Highly knowledgeable students with low reading ability can even compensate for the latter at the level of the text-base model and improve overall comprehension of a text (Recht & Leslie, 1988), but still experience some difficulties in making inferences at the level of the situation model. On the other hand, increased knowledge in students with high reading ability operates more directly at the level of the situation model, deepening understanding even more so than in the case of high-knowledge low ability readers. In sum, these results show that background knowledge is very important to achieve deep text comprehension besides well-developed reading ability (see also van Bergen et al., 2018, 2021).

We can now easily see from the previous sections that students' deep reading comprehension won't improve unless we also pay serious attention to building their background knowledge, or "word and world knowledge" (Hirsch, 2003). Yet in reading instruction, despite the fact that deep reading (and listening) comprehension requires students to make inferences that depend heavily on background knowledge, much teaching time is devoted to generic reading strategy instruction depicted as 'inferencing skills', such as finding the main idea of a text based upon signal words, to boost reading comprehension (see Sect. 2.2 for a broader discussion on the origin of these ideas). However, besides the clear initial value in practicing these comprehension strategies (Hattie, 2023; Willingham & Lovette, 2014), the same research base has equally shown that after an initial surge, the effects of reading strategy instruction on students' reading comprehension quickly reach a plateau, and have little further impact (Elleman, 2017; Rosenshine & Meister, 1994; Stevens et al., 2019; for a full overview see Willingham, 2023). That is because the goal of comprehension strategies is to activate students' background knowledge. However, if the relevant background knowledge is lacking, conscious comprehension strategies cannot activate it. Recent research has highlighted that the effects of reading strategy instruction are therefore significantly strengthened by instruction in background knowledge (Peng et al., 2023), and that the relation between knowledge and reading is indeed bidirectional and positive throughout the elementary years: in other words "knowledge begets reading, which begets knowledge" (Hwang et al., 2023).

A distinct approach to reading instruction therefore argues that, besides a focus on fluent reading ability, more content-rich instruction time in school should be dedicated to the well-thought out and balanced accumulation of background knowledge to allow better reading comprehension (Cabell & Hwang, 2020; Cervetti & Hiebert, 2019; Hirsch, 2003, Hirsch, 2016; Hwang & Duke, 2020; Neuman et al., 2014; Willingham, 2006; Willingham, 2017; Willingham & Lovette, 2014). As described in the previous section, it is important to underline, however, that building background knowledge "[…] is not just accumulating facts; rather, children need to develop knowledge networks, comprised of clusters of concepts that are coherent, generative, and supportive of future learning in a domain" (Neuman et al., 2014, p. 147). Reading and listening to different expository and narrative texts on the same subject for extended periods of time, and talking about the information and concepts they contain, can boost reading comprehension and vocabulary in the classroom (Hirsch, 2003; Wright et al., 2022). This could be particularly helpful for disadvantaged students, who depend mostly on schools to be exposed to advanced vocabulary and rich content knowledge (Hart & Risley, 2003; Hirsch, 2006; Willingham, 2017), whereas more advantaged students might improve more rapidly thanks to the language boost and solid knowledge base they receive outside the school environment, the so-called Matthew effect (Kaefer et al., 2015; Pfost et al., 2014; Rigney, 2010; Stanovich, 1986). Moreover, the often challenging transition for students from 'learning to read' to 'reading to learn' from the fourth-grade onwards is often associated with the fact that, besides problems related to coding and fluency skills (Goodwin, 2011), particularly disadvantaged students might lack sufficient background knowledge to really grasp the meaning of the expository texts they increasingly need to read in school to learn about all kinds of important topics in different subjects (Chall & Jacobs, 2003; Willingham, 2017). These text types are particularly demanding, as their informative nature builds on readers' knowledge of specific topics (Beck & McKeown, 1991). A common knowledge base, built systematically and cumulatively in school from an early age onwards, could address many of these challenges, while at the same time ensuring deep learning experiences for all students, in line with the findings from cognitive psychology research as described above.

Up until now we have focused on the importance of knowledge for learning and the acquisition of complex cognitive skills such as critical thinking and reading comprehension. In what follows, we will discuss how the current situation came about with reflections of a sociological nature on the role of knowledge in education over the years (Sect. 2.2), followed by an account of its importance from a democratic and emancipatory viewpoint (Sect. 2.3).

2.2   Knowledge Matters: A Sociological Perspective

In section two, we take a sociological perspective into why and how knowledge has been displaced in education. Starting with different views on knowledge, we further explain how constructivist and neoliberal sentiments have changed the role of knowledge. We then introduce a new line of thought that shows how to bring knowledge back into education.

2.2.1   From Objectivist to Constructivist Thinking Perspectives

Knowledge has often been associated with concepts such as 'truth', 'fact', 'social inequality', and 'class differences'. These topics gained significant attention during the early 1970s when the New Sociology of Education (NSOE) emerged. During this period, concerns regarding social class and distributional effects in education became increasingly evident. In this century, we can assume that a so-called "objectivist" (sometimes also referred to as positivist or instructivist) view of knowledge was more prevalent. Objectivism views knowledge as independent of individual and social contexts, devoid of value judgments, and purely objective. The statement 3 + 2 = 5 is a fact. That Michelangelo created frescoes on the ceiling of the Sistine Chapel in Rome is a fact. That the natural behaviour of a body is to stay in the same place or to move in a straight line at a constant speed and, without outside influences, a body's motion preserves its status is a fact (hard science). Objectivists emphasise the development of comprehensive theories and universally applicable knowledge, aiming to uncover 'absolute truths' about the world. However, this perspective has been criticised for neglecting the social dimension of knowledge, which can potentially lead to an absolutist stance that asserts universal truths without considering their situatedness and potential biases. One of the new concerns on the objectivistic view the New Sociologists brought to the fore in the 1970s was the social differentiation in education and the reproduction of social inequalities that were associated with the exclusionary structures of educational knowledge. Who had access to the knowledge of the powerful? Did a child from a working-class family acquire the same knowledge as one with highly educated parents? From this time onwards, sociologists have posited a connection between the organisation of knowledge in schools and broader social inequalities and power dynamics.

Authors such as Michael Young criticised these exclusive knowledge systems (Young, 1971) by uncovering their intimate connections to social class structures. The knowledge taught in schools was considered a tool to reinforce the dominance of the ruling social group and its perspectives. For instance, knowledge of the history and reign of the Tudors was seen as interesting and valuable for a particular ruling class in charge of society, while knowledge of how to make concrete was seen as inferior to that of the liberal arts. For this reason, the New Sociology of Education sought to uncover the hidden interests lying beneath the surface of educational knowledge and how it was taught (Moore, 2007). Over the years that followed, this perspective evolved and found expression in various theories about what happens when learning takes place (e.g. constructivism), and about what can be known (e.g. postmodernism).

Radical constructivists assert that knowledge is constructed from and deeply embedded within an individual's social and cultural environment. Isaac Newton's first law of motion acquires meaning because learners connect the new information to their prior (folk?) experiences of motion ('the ball on the grassy field did not move until I kicked it!'). They emphasise the role of human agency in shaping knowledge, recognising that it is influenced by societal norms, cultural perspectives, and individual experiences, and thus knowledge can only be constructed in a particular social context.

A postmodern perspective takes this further and states that "objective truth" is nothing more than the dominant viewpoints of the powerful elite among the variety of human experiences and the multitude of perspectives. However, these views on knowledge run the risk of relativism, where *all* knowledge is considered subjective and context-specific, potentially undermining the possibility of grounding knowledge in any objective truth. The problem that arises from this line of thinking is that it reduces knowledge to its context and the knowers that possess it. This shift in conceptualising knowledge resulted in the abandonment of knowledge as 'truth' or 'fact' to knowledge as nothing more than the viewpoints of typically dominant social groups. This also shifts the validation of knowledge from the content itself to the identity of the knower. Knowledge is no longer considered objective or neutral, but is seen as a tool the oppressive elite uses for political control. Although the absolute objectivist notion of knowledge was abandoned long ago, constructivist and postmodern views on knowledge have found fertile ground in education (Moore, 2013), both in thinking about what we want our children to learn (content) and in how we want to achieve this (teaching).

It is important to note, however, that these changes in the role of knowledge in education are much older than the 1970s. As Hirsch (2016) persuasively argues, these changes have roots in the romantic movement (eighteenth century) with the ideas of Wordsworth and Hegel that inspired Dewey, whose ideas then became a part of the so-called progressive movement in the US around 1920. The trends in the 1970s represent one of the latest continuations of these forms of thought, which have now garnered considerable influence.

2.2.2 Skills for the Twenty-first Century and Neoliberal Influences

These tendencies were amplified with the rise of neoliberalism. The focus of education shifted from cultural and civic socialisation towards a focus on employability and economic growth (Meyer & Benavot, 2013). Although almost two centuries earlier Herbert Spencer (1861) had already argued for a utilitarian and practical business-oriented education, this recent change can be attributed to the impact of globalisation and the need for nations to design their educational systems and curriculum as tools for economic development, and even national competitiveness (Yates & Young, 2010). This led to the abandonment of the idea of education as a goal in itself and shifted the focus to skills and competencies (a term borrowed from human resource management terminology) that students could later employ in the labour market. As argued by Wheelahan et al. (2022), the shift towards prioritising skills in education is rooted in human capital theory. Initially descriptive, emphasising the link between education and jobs, it evolved into a normative stance, asserting education should focus on employability. By the 2000s, it had become prescriptive, demanding education to align with workforce needs, leading to government policies shaping and funding education accordingly.

The call for developing skills relevant to the twenty-first century is the latest form of this trend (Rotherham & Willingham, 2010), and can be traced back to 2003, when the twentieth anniversary of an influential report (A Nation at Risk, 1983) triggered numerous analyses of the progress of American education. The introduction of *new* fundamental skills was recommended, including computer literacy, and various generic—and by the authors considered transferable—cognitive skills, such as critical thinking and problem-solving. However, as shown in Sect. 2.1, complex cognitive thinking skills such as critical thinking, communicating, working together (i.e., collaborating) and problem-solving are not only grounded in knowledge, but have also been key components of human progress throughout history. This is evident from early advancements in astronomy and mathematics in antiquity, such as the development of alphabets and writing, the construction of the Egyptian pyramids, and the development of Greek philosophical thought, to scientific progress in the Middle Ages, including Avicenna's early medical practices and Johannes Gutenberg's invention of the printing press using movable type to name but a few. The main difference with the skill movement was that these skills should now become universal, and not be left to chance for the happy few. Private industry and labour market economists have played a significant role in advocating for competencies such as complex thinking and communication skills (Levy & Murnane, 2013). At the start of the millennium, the top skills demanded by the most prominent and most influential companies in the United States had shifted from traditional skills such as reading, writing, and mathematics to complex skills like 'teamwork', 'critical thinking', 'problem-solving', and 'interpersonal abilities'. By 2015, the interest in the so-called twenty-first-century skills had become a global phenomenon, as evidenced by the contribution of the World Economic Forum, which outlined 16 essential proficiencies for education in the twenty-first century (see Table 2.1).

This economic undertone is also strongly reinforced by international educational policy actors, such as the European Union with its European Qualification Framework, which allows cross-country comparison of skills; the Programme for International Student Assessment (PISA) led by the OECD to assess selected student competencies; and professional training programs led by UNESCO (Mulder et al.,

Table 2.1 World economic forum—education for the twenty-first century (adapted from Scheerens et al. (2020)

Foundation literacies	Literacy and numeracy; scientific literacy, ICT literacy, financial literacy, cultural literacy, civic literacy
Competencies	Critical thinking, problem-solving, communication, collaboration
Character qualities	Creativity, initiative, persistence, grit, adaptability, curiosity, leadership, social and cultural awareness

2007, as cited in Goudard et al., 2020). While these competencies often require a foundation in domain-specific knowledge, expectations frequently overlook this requirement. They are commonly depicted as generic abilities that, when mastered, can work in a wide range of situations. Some arguments surrounding this trend ('Give a man a fish, and you feed him for a day. Teach a man to fish, and you feed him for a lifetime') even suggest that the sheer volume of new knowledge being generated diminishes the importance of actual content; it posits that the means of acquiring information have become more crucial than the information itself. This leads some to claim that as knowledge dates so quickly, teaching is no longer valuable (De Bruyckere et al., 2015). These claims also underestimate the extent to which knowledge is required to make sense of answers provided by new powerful AI-driven technologies such as ChatGPT. Information in itself, though, does not equate to understanding that information.

One can, for example, ask ChatGPT to "describe the decisive moment in the 2003 Rugby World Cup Final". The answer: '*In the dying moments of the first half of extra time, England was awarded a penalty in front of the posts. Jonny Wilkinson, England's fly-half, stepped up and successfully kicked the drop goal, securing three points for England. This iconic moment occurred with just 26 s left on the clock, propelling England into a 20–17 lead*' will, however, not make much sense unless one has some background knowledge of the sport, including what a drop-goal is, what a fly-half is, and what extra time means. Moreover, it is incorrect as the decisive moment actually came in the second period of extra time, when, with 30 s remaining, Wilkinson kicked a drop goal (not a penalty kick) to break the 17–17 tie. Consequently, knowledge is also required to know whether an answer is likely to be correct, reflects biases (such as has been the case in, for example, depictions of people of different ethnicities), or is even simply the result of a so-called AI hallucination (as in this particular case). This all leads to concerns that an exaggerated emphasis on generalised 21st-century skills, and a blind trust in technology conflict with our understanding of human learning as described above, and may fail to adequately serve students—particularly those from disadvantaged backgrounds—grappling with social inequity (Rotherham & Willingham, 2010).

All of the above, however, does not mean that education should not have any links to employment (as we will discuss below), nor that complex thinking skills are not important; they very much are. Rather, it underscores the necessity of recognising that domain-specific knowledge is crucial when imparting skills to students, and that generalised lessons on, for instance, critical thinking are not that productive. In this sense, we need to bring knowledge back in.

2.2.3 Bringing Knowledge Back in

At the onset of this century, a group of scholars, self-identifying as social realists, expressed discontent with these trends, asserting that they had downgraded knowledge in education (Barrett, 2024). This downgrading denies learners access to what they call *powerful knowledge,* which most often affects students from disadvantaged backgrounds the most (Wheelahan, 2010). For this reason, they argued for the need to 'bring knowledge back in' (Muller, 2000; Rata, 2012; Wheelahan, 2007; Young, 2007). Taking a realist perspective, they recognise the social nature of knowledge in its production (which withholds it from absolutism) yet reject the reduction of knowledge to knowers (which counters relativism). They do this by acknowledging that some knowledge is more objective than others in ways that transcend the immediate conditions of its production (Moore & Young, 2001). In other words, while knowledge is socially produced, some types of knowledge are more powerful, and, yes, 'better', than others. With this *better* knowledge, however, it is not meant that it is beyond debate, or that it is fixed. "Better knowledge means the best knowledge we have, and the best means we have for creating new knowledge for the kind of world we envisage for the next generation" (Young & Lambert, 2014, p. 31). Based on this idea and the theories of Bernstein and Durkheim, Michael Young (2009, 2013) produced a theory of *powerful knowledge.* He positions the production of powerful knowledge within specific social and intellectual groups, often represented by academic disciplines. This disciplinary knowledge holds more power as compared to everyday knowledge because it is produced in "communities of inquiry" that use specific methods to create and validate claims of knowledge (Young & Muller, 2015). In this context, academic disciplines such as mathematics, physics, and history are valuable because they can generate focused discussions that ensure reliability, revisability, and the emergence of new insights (Muller & Young, 2019).

The powers of disciplinary knowledge reside in going beyond individual experiences, providing individuals with a robust framework to understand the world. For example, it can help students understand that the Earth is round, a realisation that goes beyond the visual appearance of a seemingly flat horizon. Although this concept may seem profound to new learners, the underlying geometry and arithmetic are surprisingly straightforward. The ancient Greek mathematician Eratosthenes ingeniously demonstrated this almost two and a half millennia ago. By observing differences in the shadows cast by vertical objects at the same moment in different locations on Earth, Eratosthenes not only inferred the curvature of the Earth, but also calculated its circumference. Rooted in fundamental geometry and arithmetic, his calculations provided compelling evidence for a spherical Earth. Disciplinary knowledge thus provides learners with more dependable interpretations and insights into the world, allowing them to explore topics and subjects their experiences alone would never let them have access to. It also serves as a language that allows individuals to question its own foundations and the authorities from which it derives. The acquisition of disciplinary knowledge enables individuals to envision alternative possibilities and think beyond the confines of their immediate surroundings.

For these reasons, Young advocates inclusive access to powerful knowledge in education, asserting equal educational rights for all children. He argues that if 'better knowledge' exists, everyone should have the right to access it (Young & Lambert, 2014). This does not mean that powerful knowledge is the silver bullet for all our problems, and that we should just start teaching the 'best' knowledge in our disciplines and everything will be alright. Muller (2023) points out that this is expecting too much from the concept. What constitutes powerful knowledge changes as disciplinary knowledge itself evolves; in some areas, such as environmental science, quite rapidly (Yan, 2015). Furthermore, what counts as powerful knowledge in particular disciplines, such as history, is itself subject to debate, and contextually differentiated (Sheehan, 2021). For these reasons it is important to clarify that this perspective does not assert the presence of an unchanging or universally accepted canonical knowledge across disciplines. It is also important to point out that disciplinary knowledge in the academic disciplines themselves on the one hand, and disciplinary knowledge in schools on the other, are two different things. Disciplinary knowledge in the disciplines needs to be translated by expert teachers and subject specialists. While powerful knowledge cannot serve as a silver bullet, it can help us as a future-oriented principle where we strive towards a more desirable future and reappreciate knowledge and the emancipatory and democratic qualities it brings.

2.3 Knowledge Matters: A Democratic Perspective

In a democratic society devoted to equal opportunities and governance for and by the people, one of our democratic responsibilities, namely deciding what our children should know, is complex. What we know plays a significant role in shaping our identities and who we are, or are perceived to be (Moore, 2000). Deciding what our children should learn does not only play a role in what we want the future of our society to be like, but also in who we want our children to become. This leads us to a very difficult question: What kind of knowledge is so important that we will not leave its transmission up to chance? A question that becomes ever more difficult to answer as the production of knowledge in our society grows. One could argue that the response to this question depends heavily on the answer to a different question: what is the purpose of education? While there are many possible answers, most can be divided into four broad categories: **personal empowerment, cultural transmission, preparation for work,** and **preparation for citizenship** (Wiliam, 2013). These broad philosophies do not exclude one another but are sometimes in conflict. A balance is needed, as one without the other can have unwanted consequences.

For example, an education system focused only on preparation for work could lead to an instrumentalist view where only knowledge that is considered "useful" for economic growth is taught. Such an instrumentalist view might overlook the intrinsic value of knowledge for personal empowerment and cultural transmission and diminish the broader benefits that a well-rounded education can bring. It also lends itself to the inference that employers should have a significant voice in deciding what children learn, and it's not obvious that they would wield this power in a way that benefits society as a whole.

The knowledge and skills we *think* everyone will need for further economic development could also be misguided, since we don't have a crystal ball to tell us what the future holds. On the other hand, an educational system solely focused on personal empowerment might lead to a disconnect between the knowledge and skills taught in schools and what students need to function in the labour market upon which our societal prosperity relies. Discovering and maintaining this balance and determining what should be taught is a project that never ends, given that an effective system today may prove inadequate in the future as society changes. However, choices need to be made. In the next paragraphs, we will take a closer look at the aim of preparing our children for citizenship in a democratic society and how knowledge plays an important role in this process.

When examining knowledge from a democratic perspective, one cannot overlook the ideas of E.D. Hirsch and his notions of cultural literacy. Hirsch (1988, p. xiii) defined being culturally literate as "possessing the basic information needed to thrive in the modern world". With this concept, he pointed out the **significance of background knowledge in language comprehension,** and how disadvantaged students rely primarily on schools to provide this knowledge. As explained in the first section, student's already acquired knowledge (we refer to this as 'background' knowledge) acts as a cognitive scaffold, enabling students to connect added information and their pre-existing understanding of the world. When communicating, we assume a vast amount of shared background knowledge. For disadvantaged students, who may face limitations in exposure to a rich array of experiences and information outside schools, this can limit them, not due to a lack of ability, but because of a lack of access to knowledge (remember the scorpion in the section on reading comprehension?).

This is why, when knowledge is no longer explicitly addressed in schools, or assumed to be primarily constructed from children's own experiences, the most disadvantaged students suffer the most. This is problematic not only for these individuals but also for society as a whole. As Hirsch (2009) states, shared knowledge fosters a sense of commonality among diverse citizens in a democratic society. In a society characterised by cultural diversity, a common body of knowledge ensures that citizens can engage in informed discussions, debates, and decision-making processes. It promotes a sense of belonging and inclusivity, as individuals draw upon shared references that go beyond individual differences. One can imagine that when access to this shared knowledge is hindered or not evenly distributed, issues of inequality in education may widen. This is why the erosion of the role of knowledge within the educational landscape can have dire consequences (Hirsch, 2016).

Hirsch's ideas have significantly influenced the resurgence of and emphasis on knowledge as a vital component of society and education. Nevertheless, his ideas have been criticised due to their perceived traditional and conservative nature. Social realists such as Michael Young share Hirsch's views on the importance of knowledge in our society and its vital role in education. Yet, these social realists relocate (powerful) knowledge within academic disciplines, making what is taught and learned in classrooms more reflective of the characteristics of disciplinary knowledge developed by specialist communities. They also share Hirsch's view on knowledge as a prerequisite for fostering equitable opportunities for all and for social justice. Leesa Wheelahan (2010) further strengthens this viewpoint from a democratic perspective, emphasising the crucial role of disciplinary knowledge in granting individuals access to society's ongoing conversation about itself. Providing access to disciplinary knowledge is crucial for an effective democracy, as it allows societies to contemplate the 'not-yet-thought and unthinkable' and fosters the imagination of alternative futures (Bernstein, 2000). Disciplinary knowledge is the result of a global learning process. Young echoes this sentiment and argues that disciplinary, *powerful* knowledge empowers learners to go beyond their own experiences. It also arms them with the language to participate in discussions on politics, morality, environmentalism, migration, and many other topics prevalent in civil society. Furthermore, it also gives them the capacity to scrutinise the foundations of knowledge, the authority upon which it stands, and thus, the tools to be critical of it (Young, 2007). Let us illustrate this with the following excerpt from a fictitious news article:

> *The struggle over this aid forms a growing obstacle to progress in negotiations during climate summits. As long as wealthy countries do not provide the assistance they have pledged, many poor countries are unwilling to do more to reduce their greenhouse gas emissions. According to most experts, emissions will rise rapidly in poor countries and emerging economies.*

Not only do the authors of this article expect much broad background knowledge from their readership, but also a good understanding of domain-specific knowledge. Why are greenhouse gases such a problem? Is this a valid claim and why? If this is true, why do poorer countries not want to reduce them if rich countries do not assist? As previously discussed in the section on reading comprehension, even if the reader can successfully decode and read this article, much more is needed to deeply comprehend it and contribute meaningfully to the discussion. This is why, as Wheelahan (2010) argues, disciplinary knowledge is socially powerful knowledge. Students need knowledge to be able to participate in societal debates. This does not mean that every child needs to become a mathematician or historian, but they do need access to a foundation of disciplinary knowledge to be able to reason and develop an understanding of how that knowledge is used and validated in debates. However, this extends beyond merely theoretical debates. It applies equally, for example, to workers who require access to disciplinary knowledge that supports their professional practice. Today, a car mechanic needs to understand theoretical automotive engineering concepts, such as combustion engines, electronic systems, and diagnostic techniques. If mechanics only rely on practical experience without digging into the underlying theory, they might find it challenging to troubleshoot and adapt to advancements in vehicle technology. While practical experience remains extremely important, theoretical knowledge equips them with the insights needed to understand new technologies, discuss industry developments, and meaningfully contribute to conversations on automotive innovation.

While deciding what knowledge ought to be provided to our children will (and should!) always be the result of societal debate, ensuring that knowledge itself is not forgotten is crucial for equitable opportunities for all and our democratic society. Hirsch has shown us the importance of a common knowledge base and helped bring knowledge back into the conversation, whereas social realism has brought knowledge back into social theory, while at the same time emphasising the importance of the disciplinary aspect of knowledge.

2.4 How Knowledge Matters Summarised

Our perspective on knowledge is shaped by the lens through which we view it. From a cognitive psychology standpoint, the value of a well-established knowledge base for learning, and complex cognitive skills such as critical thinking and reading comprehension is unequivocally recognised. We now know that humans have the capacity to construct a robust knowledge base within long-term memory, that provides us with the resources to enhance the efficacy of working memory during cognitive tasks. When examining knowledge from various perspectives, it is evident that its significance has been subject to fluctuating societal trends, and that those societal viewpoints have at times overshadowed the importance of knowledge. Revitalised by contemporary democratic and social perspectives, and bolstered by consistent findings from cognitive psychology, we are now witnessing a revival of the importance of knowledge in education. It has now re-emerged as a prerequisite for improved learning, critical thinking, and deep reading comprehension, as a facilitator for collective discourse, and as a catalyst for equitable opportunities for all. All these aspects have implications for the curriculum, which is at the heart of the third part of this publication.

References

A Nation at Risk the Imperative for Educational Reform. (1983). A Report to the Nation and the Secretary of Education, United States Department of Education. Washington, D.C. National Commission on Excellence in Education. [Superintendent of Documents, U.S. Government Printing Office distributor].

Alexander, P., Kulikowich, J., & Schulze, S. (1994). How subject-matter knowledge affects recall and interest. *American Educational Research Journal, 31*(2), 313–337.

Atkinson, R. C., & Shiffrin, R. M. (1968). Human memory: A proposed system and its control processes. In *Psychology of learning and motivation* (Vol. 2, pp. 89–195). Academic press.

Ausubel, D. P. (1968). *Educational psychology: A cognitive view.* Holt, Rinehart and Winston, Inc.

Ayres, P. L. (1993). Why goal-free problems can facilitate learning. *Contemporary Educational Psychology, 18*(3), 376–381.

Baddeley, A., & Hitch, G. (1974). Working memory. In G. H. Bower (Ed.), *The psychology of learning and motivation: Advances in research and theory* (Vol. 8, pp. 47–89). Academic Press.

Baddeley, A. D., & Andrade, J. (2000). Working memory and the vividness of imagery. *Journal of Experimental Psychology: General, 129*, 126–145.

Barrett, B. (2024). Rob moore, social realism, and the sociology of education and knowledge. In Rata, E. (Ed.), *Research handbook in curriculum and education*, Chap. 5 (pp. 79–87). Edward Elgar Publishing.

Beck, I. L., & McKeown, M. G. (1991). Research directions: Social studies texts are hard to understand: Mediating some of the difficulties. *Language Arts, 68*(6), 482–490.

Bernstein, B. (2000). *Pedagogy, symbolic control, and identity: Theory, research, critique* (Vol. 5). Rowman & Littlefield.

Broadbent, D. (1958). *Perception and communication.* Pergamon Press. https://doi.org/10.1037/10037-000

Brod, G. (2021). Toward an understanding of when prior knowledge helps or hinders learning. *npj Science of Learning, 6*(1), 24.

Cabell, S. Q., & Hwang, H. (2020). Building content knowledge to boost comprehension in the primary grades. *Reading Research Quarterly, 55*, 99–107.

Carver, R. P. (1994). Percentage of unknown vocabulary words in text as a function of the relative difficulty of the text: Implications for instruction. *Journal of Reading Behavior, 26*(4), 413–437.

Castles, A., Rastle, K., & Nation, K. (2018). Ending the reading wars: Reading acquisition from novice to expert. *Psychological Science in the Public Interest, 19*(1), 5–51.

Cervetti, G. N., & Hiebert, E. H. (2019). Knowledge at the center of English language arts instruction. *The Reading Teacher, 72*(4), 499–507.

Chall, J. S., & Jacobs, V. A. (2003). The classic study on poor children's fourth-grade slump. *American Educator, 27*(1), 14–44.

Csikszentmihalyi, M. (1990). *Flow: The psychology of optimal experience*. Harper and Row.

De Bruyckere, K., Kirschner, P. A., & Hulshof, C. D. (2015). *Urban myths about learning and education*. Elsevier.

De Bruyckere, P., Kirschner, P. A., & Hulshof, C. D. (2020). If you learn A, will you be better able to learn B? Understanding transfer of learning. *American Educator, 44*, 30–34.

Ehri, L. C., Nunes, S. R., Willows, D. M., Schuster, B. V., Yaghoub-Zadeh, Z., & Shanahan, T. (2001). Phonemic awareness instruction helps children learn to read: Evidence from the National Reading Panel's meta-analysis. *Reading Research Quarterly, 36*(3), 250–287.

Elleman, A. M. (2017). Examining the impact of inference instruction on the literal and inferential comprehension of skilled and less skilled readers: A meta-analytic review. *Journal of Educational Psychology, 109*(6), 761–781.

Elleman, A. M., Lindo, E. J., Morphy, P., & Compton, D. L. (2009). The impact of vocabulary instruction on passage-level comprehension of school-age children: A meta-analysis. *Journal of Research on Educational Effectiveness, 2*(1), 1–44.

Geary, D. C. (2011). Cognitive predictors of achievement growth in mathematics: A 5-year longitudinal study. *Developmental Psychology, 47*(6), 1539.

Geary, D., & Berch, D. (2016). Evolution and children's cognitive and academic development. In D. Geary & D. Berch (Eds.), *Evolutionary perspectives on child development and education* (pp. 217–249). Springer.

Gick, M. L., & Holyoak, K. J. (1983). Schema induction and analogical transfer. *Cognitive Psychology, 15*(1), 1–38.

Goodwin, B. (2011). Don't wait until 4th grade to address the slump. *Educational Leadership, 68*(7), 88–89.

Goudard, P., Pont, B., & Viennet, R. (2020). Education responses to COVID-19: Implementing a way forward. *OECD Education Working Papers*.

Graham, S., & Santangelo, T. (2014). Does spelling instruction make students better spellers, readers, and writers? A meta-analytic review. *Reading and Writing, 27*, 1703–1743.

De Groot, A. (1965). *Thought and choice in chess*. Mouton Publishers.

Hart, B., & Risley, T. R. (2003). The early catastrophe: The 30 million word gap by age 3. *American Educator, 27*(1), 4–9.

Hattie, J. (2023). *Visible learning: The sequel: A synthesis of over 2,100 meta-analyses relating to achievement*. Taylor & Francis.

Hirsch, E. D. (1988). *Cultural literacy: What every American needs to know*. Vintage.

Hirsch, E. D. (2006). *The knowledge deficit*. Houghton Mifflin.

Hirsch, E. D. (2009). *The making of Americans: Democracy and our schools*. Yale University Press.

Hirsch, E. D. (2016). *Why knowledge matters: Rescuing our children from failed educational theories*. Harvard Education Press.

Hirsch, E. D. (2003). Reading comprehension requires knowledge of words and the world. *American Educator, 27*, 10–13.

Hsueh-Chao, M. H., & Nation, P. (2000). Unknown vocabulary density and reading comprehension. *Reading in a Foreign Language, 13*(1), 403–430.

Hwang, H., & Duke, N. K. (2020). Content counts and motivation matters: Reading comprehension in third-grade students who are English learners. *AERA Open, 6*(1).

Hwang, H., McMaster, K. L., & Kendeou, P. (2023). A longitudinal investigation of directional relations between domain knowledge and reading in the elementary years. *Reading Research Quarterly, 58*(1), 59–77.

Kaefer, T., Neuman, S. B., & Pinkham, A. M. (2015). Pre-existing background knowledge influences socioeconomic differences in preschoolers' word learning and comprehension. *Reading Psychology, 36*(3), 203–231.

Kapur, M. (2008). Productive failure. *Cognition and instruction, 26*(3), 379–424.

Kendeou, P., & Van Den Broek, P. (2007). The effects of prior knowledge and text structure on comprehension processes during reading of scientific texts. *Memory & Cognition, 35*(7), 1567–1577.

Kintsch, W. (1998). *Comprehension: A paradigm for cognition.* Cambridge University Press.

Kintsch, W., & van Dijk, T. A. (1978). Toward a model of text comprehension and production. *Psychological Review, 85*(5), 363–394.

Kirschner, P. A. (1991). *Practicals in higher science education.* [Doctoral Thesis, Open Universiteit: faculties and services]. Open Universiteit

Kirschner, P. A., & De Bruyckere, P. (2017). The myths of the digital native and the multitasker. *Teaching and Teacher Education, 67*, 135–142.

Laufer, B. (1992). How much lexis is necessary for reading comprehension? In *Vocabulary and applied linguistics* (pp. 126–132). Palgrave Macmillan UK.

Laufer, B., & Yano, Y. (2001). Understanding unfamiliar words in a text: Do L2 learners understand how much they don't understand? *Reading in a Foreign Language, 13*(2), 549–566.

Levy, F., & Murnane, R. (2013). Dancing with robots: Human skills for computerized work. http://www.thirdway.org/report/dancing-with-robots-human-skills-for-computerized-work

Lin, X., & Powell, S. R. (2022). The roles of initial mathematics, reading, and cognitive skills in subsequent mathematics performance: A meta-analytic structural equation modeling approach. *Review of Educational Research, 92*(2), 288–325.

McCarthy, K. S., & McNamara, D. S. (2021). The multidimensional knowledge in text comprehension framework. *Educational Psychologist., 56*(3), 196–214.

Meyer, H. D., & Benavot, A. (Eds.). (2013). *PISA, power, and policy: The emergence of global educational governance.* Symposium Books Ltd.

Miller, G. A. (1957). Some effects of intermittent silence. *The American Journal of Psychology, 70*(2), 311–314.

Moore, R. (2000). For knowledge: Tradition, progressivism and progress in education—reconstructing the curriculum debate. *Cambridge Journal of Education, 30*(1), 17–36.

Moore, R. (2007). Going critical: The problem of problematizing knowledge in education studies. *Critical Studies in Education, 48*(1), 25–41.

Moore, R. (2013). Social realism and the problem of knowledge in the sociology of education. *British Journal of Sociology of Education, 34*(3), 333–353.

Moore, R., & Young, M. (2001). Knowledge and the curriculum in the sociology of education: Towards a reconceptualisation. *British Journal of Sociology of Education, 22*(4), 445–461.

Mulder, M., Weigel, T., & Collins, K. (2007). The concept of competence in the development of vocational education and training in selected EU member states: A critical analysis. *Journal of Vocational Education and Training, 59*(1), 67–88.

Muller, J. (2000). *Reclaiming knowledge. Social theory, curriculum and education policy.* Routledge.

Muller, J. (2023). Powerful knowledge, disciplinary knowledge, curriculum knowledge: Educational knowledge in question. *International Research in Geographical and Environmental Education, 32*(1), 20–34.

Muller, J., & Young, M. (2019). Knowledge, power and powerful knowledge re-visited. *The Curriculum Journal, 30*(2), 196–214.

Nation, K., & Snowling, M. J. (1998). Semantic processing and the development of word-recognition skills: Evidence from children with reading comprehension difficulties. *Journal of Memory and Language, 39*(1), 85–101.

Nation, P. (2001). *Learning vocabulary in another language.* Cambridge: Cambridge University Press.

National Reading Panel (U.S.) & National Institute of Child Health and Human Development (U.S.). (2000). Report of the national reading panel: Teaching children to read: an evidence-based assessment of the scientific research literature on reading and its implications for reading instruction. U.S. Dept. of Health and Human Services, Public Health Service, National Institutes of Health, National Institute of Child Health and Human Development.

National Research Council. (2000). *How people learn: Brain, mind, experience, and school*: Expanded edition. National Academies Press.

Neuman, S. B., Kaefer, T., & Pinkham, A. (2014). Building background knowledge. *The Reading Teacher, 68*(2), 145–148.

Oakhill, J., Cain, K., McCarthy, D., & Nightingale, Z. (2012). Making the link between vocabulary knowledge and comprehension skill. In M. A. Britt, S. R. Goldman, & J. F. Rouet (Eds.), *Reading: From words to multiple texts* (pp. 101–114). New York: Routledge.

OECD. (2024). *New PISA results on creative thinking: Can students think outside the box?* PISA in Focus, No. 125, OECD Publishing.

Ouellette, G. P. (2006). What's meaning got to do with it: The role of vocabulary in word reading and reading comprehension. *Journal of Educational Psychology, 98*(3), 554–566.

Pearson, P. D., & Cervetti, G. (2015). Fifty years of reading comprehension theory and practice. In P. D. Pearson & E. H. Hiebert (Eds.), *Research-based practices for teaching common core literacy.* Teachers College, Columbia University.

Peng, P., Wang, W., Filderman, M. J., Zhang, W., & Lin, L. (2023). The active ingredient in reading comprehension strategy intervention for struggling readers: A bayesian network meta-analysis. *Review of Educational Research*, 003465432311171345.

Perfetti, C. (2007). Reading ability: Lexical quality to comprehension. *Scientific Studies of Reading, 11*(4), 357–383.

Pfost, M., Hattie, J., Dörfler, T., & Artelt, C. (2014). Individual differences in reading development: A review of 25 years of empirical research on Matthew effects in reading. *Review of Educational Research, 84*(2), 203–244.

RAND Reading Study Group. (2002). *Reading for understanding: Toward a research and development program in reading comprehension.* Santa Monica, CA: RAND Corporation.

Rata, E. (2012). The politics of knowledge in education. *British Educational Research Journal, 38*, 103–124.

Recht, D. R., & Leslie, L. (1988). Effect of prior knowledge on good and poor readers' memory of text. *Journal of Educational Psychology, 80*(1), 16–20.

Renn, J. (2020). *The evolution of knowledge: Rethinking science for the Anthropocene.* Princeton University Press.

Rigney, D. (2010). *The Matthew effect: How advantage begets further advantage.* Columbia University Press.

Rosenshine, B., & Meister, C. (1994). Reciprocal teaching: A review of the research. *Review of Educational Research, 64*(4), 479–530.

Rotherham, A. J., & Willingham, D. T. (2010). 21st-century skills. *American Educator, 17*(1), 17–20.

Ruan, Y., Georgiou, G. K., Song, S., Li, Y., & Shu, H. (2018). Does writing system influence the associations between phonological awareness, morphological awareness, and reading? A meta-analysis. *Journal of Educational Psychology, 110*(2), 180.

Scarborough, H. S., Neuman, S., & Dickinson, D. (2009). Connecting early language and literacy to later reading (dis) abilities: Evidence, theory, and practice. *Approaching Difficulties in Literacy Development: Assessment, Pedagogy and Programmes, 10*, 23–38.

Scheerens, J., van der Werf, G., & de Boer, H. (2020). *Soft skills in education.* Springer International Publishing.

Schmitt, N., Jiang, X., & Grabe, W. (2011). The percentage of words known in a text and reading comprehension. *The Modern Language Journal, 95*(1), 26–43.

Shapiro, A. (2004). How including prior knowledge as a subject variable may change outcomes of learning research. *American Educational Research Journal, 41*(1), 159–189.

Sheehan, H. M. (2021). *Powerful subject pedagogical knowledge in teacher education and its integration into practice.* Doctoral thesis, Sheffield Hallam University.

Simonsmeier, B. A., Flaig, M., Deiglmayr, A., Schalk, L., & Schneider, M. (2022). Domain-specific prior knowledge and learning: A meta-analysis. *Educational Psychologist, 57*(1), 31–54.

Smith, R., Snow, P., Serry, T., & Hammond, L. (2021). The role of background knowledge in reading comprehension: A critical review. *Reading Psychology, 42*(3), 214–240.

Spencer, H. (1861). *Essays on education and kindred subjects.* Reprint 1911. https://www.gutenberg.org/ebooks/16510

Stanovich, K. E. (1986). Matthew effects in reading: Some consequences of individual differences in the acquisition of literacy. *Reading Research Quarterly, 21*(4), 360–407. Retrieved from http://www.psychologytoday.com/files/u81/Stanovich__1986_.pdf

Stevens, E. A., Park, S., & Vaughn, S. (2019). A review of summarizing and main idea interventions for struggling readers in grades 3 through 12: 1978–2016. *Remedial and Special Education, 40*(3), 131–149.

Thorndike, E. L. (1923). The infuence of frst-year latin upon ability to read english. *School & Society, 17*, 165–168.

Van Bergen, E., Snowling, M. J., de Zeeuw, E. L., van Beijsterveldt, C. E., Dolan, C. V., & Boomsma, D. I. (2018). Why do children read more? The influence of reading ability on voluntary reading practices. *Journal of Child Psychology and Psychiatry, 59*(11), 1205–1214.

Van Bergen, E., Vasalampi, K., & Torppa, M. (2021). How are practice and performance related? Development of reading from age 5 to 15. *Reading Research Quarterly, 56*(3), 415–434.

Van Merriënboer, J. J., & Kirschner, P. A. (2017). *Ten steps to complex learning: A systematic approach to four-component instructional design.* Routledge.

Ward, T. B., & Kolomyts, Y. (2010). Cognition and creativity. In J. C. Kaufman & R. J. Sternberg (Eds.), *Cambridge Handbook of Creativity* (pp. 93–112). New York, NY: Cambridge University Press.

Wheelahan, L. (2010). *Why knowledge matters in curriculum: A social realist argument.* Routledge.

Wheelahan, L. (2007). How competency-based training locks the working class out of powerful knowledge: A modified Bernsteinian analysis. *British Journal of Sociology of Education, 28*(5), 637–651.

Wheelahan, L., Moodie, G., & Doughney, J. (2022). Challenging the skills fetish. *British Journal of Sociology of Education, 43*(3), 475–494.

Wiliam, D. (2013). *Principled curriculum design.* SSAT (The Schools Network) Limited.

Wiliam, D. (2018). *Creating the schools our children need.* Learning Sciences International.

Willingham, D. T. (2019). How to teach critical thinking. NSW Department of Education. Retrieved from: https://education.nsw.gov.au/teaching-and-learning/education-for-a-changing-world/resource-library/how-to-teach-critical-thinking.html.

Willingham, D.T. (2021). *Why don't students like school? A cognitive scientist answers questions about how the mind works and what it means for the classroom.* John Wiley & Sons.

Willingham, D. T. (2023). Beyond comprehension. *Association for Supervision and Curriculum Development, 81*(4). Retrieved from https://www.ascd.org/el/articles/beyond-comprehension.

Willingham, D. T. (2006). How knowledge helps: It speeds and strengthens reading comprehension, learning and thinking. *American Educator, 30*(1), 30.

Willingham, D. T. (2017). *The reading mind. A cognitive approach to understanding how the mind reads.* San Francisco, CA: Jossey-Bass.

Willingham, D. T., & Lovette, G. (2014). Can reading comprehension be taught? *Teachers College Record, 116*, 1–3.

Wright, T. S., Cervetti, G. N., Wise, C., & McClung, N. A. (2022). The impact of knowledge-building through conceptually-coherent read alouds on vocabulary and comprehension. *Reading Psychology, 43*(1), 70–84.

Yan, E. (2015). Disciplinary knowledge production and diffusion in science. *Journal of the Association for Information Science and Technology, 67*(9), 2223–2245. https://doi.org/10.1002/asi.23541

Yates, L., & Young, M. (2010). Globalisation, knowledge and the curriculum. *European Journal of Education, 45*(1), 4–10.

Young, M. (1971). *Knowledge and control: New directions for the sociology of education.* Collier-Macmillan Publishers.

Young, M. (2007). *Bringing knowledge back in: From social constructivism to social realism in the sociology of education.* Routledge.

Young, M., & Lambert, D. (2014). *Knowledge and the future school. Curriculum and social justice.* Bloomsbury.

Young, M., & Muller, J. (2015). *Curriculum and the specialization of knowledge: Studies in the sociology of education.* Routledge.

Young, M. (2009). Education, globalisation and the voice of knowledge. *Journal of Education and Work, 22*(3), 193–204.

Young, M. (2013). Overcoming the crisis in curriculum theory: A knowledge-based approach. *Journal of Curriculum Studies, 45*(2), 101–108.

Zhilin, D. M. T., & Tkachuk, L. E. (2013). Chunking in chemistry. *Eurasian Journal of Physics and Chemistry Education, 5*, 39–56.

Zwaan, R. A., & Radvansky, G. A. (1998). Situation models in language comprehension and memory. *Psychological Bulletin, 123*(2), 162–185. American Psychological Association.

Chapter 3
Knowledge and the Curriculum

Abstract The curriculum is a complex concept central to educational debates. Over the years, the role of knowledge in the curriculum has, like a pendulum, shifted between two extremes, from highly visible to virtually invisible knowledge elements. In this chapter, we consider the lessons learned from both extremes, proposing a knowledge-rich curriculum as the soundest way forward to both effectively acquire knowledge and complex cognitive skills in school, but also as a crucial lever to achieve equitable opportunities for all students. In understanding how a knowledge-rich curriculum can enhance learning, three overarching principles are discussed: (1) content-richness, (2) coherence, and (3) clarity. These principles are illustrated through practical examples from schools and educators who have effectively implemented knowledge-rich curricula, and combined with insights from relevant research on curriculum studies.

Keywords Knowledge-rich · Curriculum · Knowledge acquisition · Complex cognitive skills · Curricular coherence · Curricular clarity · Content-richness · Equitable opportunities

3.1 Everything Starts with the Curriculum

In the previous sections, we discussed the importance of knowledge and how it constitutes an essential component of deep thinking. This has important implications for the curriculum in educational settings. Nuno Crato (2021) neatly highlights its utmost importance in that regard as follows:

> First, everything starts with the curriculum. This is the education founding document. It can be national, federal, regional, or established at local levels. It can be more detailed or less specific, it can be later translated in standards or contain them, but without clear learning goals no education system can progress. Second, the curriculum, or curricular structure if it is made from different pieces, ought to be ambitious, demanding, and set clear objectives. These objectives must be sequenced, setting solid foundations for students' progress. Knowledge is a necessary foundation to develop skills and values. Third, everything needs to be coherent around curricular goals. It does not make sense that assessment instruments evaluate some

learning goals, textbooks stress others, and schools are rewarded for attaining still different student goals (p. 20).

However, to state that the concept 'curriculum' is complex is at the same time quite an understatement. Formulating a definition that covers its complexity is therefore a very challenging task, akin to 'waiting for Godot'. Those readers with background knowledge on Samuel Beckett's play will have no problem understanding this comparison. This complexity is also reflected in the literature, with Ian C. Rule identifying 119 distinct definitions of curriculum in 1973 (Portelli, 1987). Some even go as far as to state that "there are as many definitions as authors" (Thijs & van den Akker, 2009, p. 9). For the sake of clarity and for the purpose of this book, however, we will define the curriculum as a 'plan for learning over time' (Taba, 1962; Thijs & van den Akker, 2009). Acknowledging that this definition still has its limitations, we believe it is important to start this section by highlighting some factors regarding the complexity of curriculum as a concept. Understanding these factors may help clarify why curriculum is at the centre of so many debates in education, and why these debates are so important.

A first factor to consider is the **broad or narrow perspective** you adopt when considering the concept 'curriculum'. Learning is not limited to what happens at school; students' social environment also plays a significant role. Think about what children could learn by joining the Scouts, taking music lessons, or playing basketball with friends at the local court, but also what their parents might teach them by taking them to museums, and the topics that are or are not discussed at the dinner table. These aspects are also referred to as the societal curriculum (Deng, 2017). In this book we focus on the content and learning activities organised at school and the system behind it (Popham & Baker, 1970; Tyler, 1949), yet we take into consideration these important factors that can influence the learning potential of students. Kerr (1968) resumes this viewpoint as follows: "All the learning which is planned or guided by the school, whether it is carried on in groups or individually inside or outside the school" (p. 16).

A second and perhaps even more important factor is the fact that curriculum depends on **a conception of education and learning**. What do we as a society, as schools, as teachers value, and what is the goal of schooling? In other words, why do students learn in school? The answer to this question also determines the emphasis placed by an educational system, individual schools, and even individual teachers. It also implies that shaping the curriculum is about making choices.

The work of Tyler (1949) provides us with valuable guidelines in this regard. He poses four fundamental questions that can provide direction in the decisions that need to be made:

- What educational purposes should the school seek to attain? (standards, curriculum philosophy, epistemology)
- What educational experiences can be provided that are likely to attain these purposes? (curriculum, instruction)
- How can these educational experiences be effectively organised? (curriculum, teaching)
- How can we determine whether these purposes are being attained? (assessment, evaluation)

Van den Akker (2003) equally emphasises this purposefulness, and stresses that every curriculum starts with a rationale with a view to student learning, upon which other factors within the educational context can be aligned. He illustrates this with the metaphor of a curricular spider web, as depicted in Fig. 3.1. In this representation, any alteration to this rationale can consequently prompt changes to various elements of the curriculum, including the provided content, the articulation of learning objectives, assessment methods, and more. This underlines the inherent complexity of curriculum, in which, similar to a spider web, "every chain is as strong as its weakest link"(p. 5).

A third factor to consider is that when it has been determined in the curriculum what we want students to learn, this does not automatically equal what students actually learn. That is due to **discrepancies** between what Bauersfeld (1979) calls *the intended curriculum* (what we want students to learn), *the implemented curriculum* (how these intended learning goals are then enacted), and *the attained curriculum* (what students actually learn). Below, we will discuss these discrepancies in more detail. On top of the discrepancy between the intended and the attained curriculum, another issue emerges regarding curriculum intentions and what students eventually learn. As Kelly (2009) points out "some educationalists speak of *the hidden curriculum*, referring to those things which students learn at school because of the way in which the school's work is planned and organised, and through the materials provided, but which are not overtly included in the planning or sometimes even in the consciousness of those responsible for the school arrangements" (p. 10). In other words, curriculum building and implementation are never neutral. Reynolds and Hattan (2024) address the latter issue from a gender viewpoint with a recent example of a unit on American presidents that clearly lacks female or other representation. What kind of implicit message is communicated with regard to certain students' possibilities to become president? And what might change if, for instance, influential Congressional representatives such as Kamala Harris, Michelle Obama, or Hillary Clinton were included in the unit? Moreover, as curriculum building is about making choices and teaching time is scarce, this implies a risk that some voices will be more present than others in the curriculum. Eisner (1985) calls this *the null curriculum*: "the options students are not afforded, the perspectives they may never know about, much less be able to use, the concepts and skills that are not part of their intellectual repertoire" (p. 107).

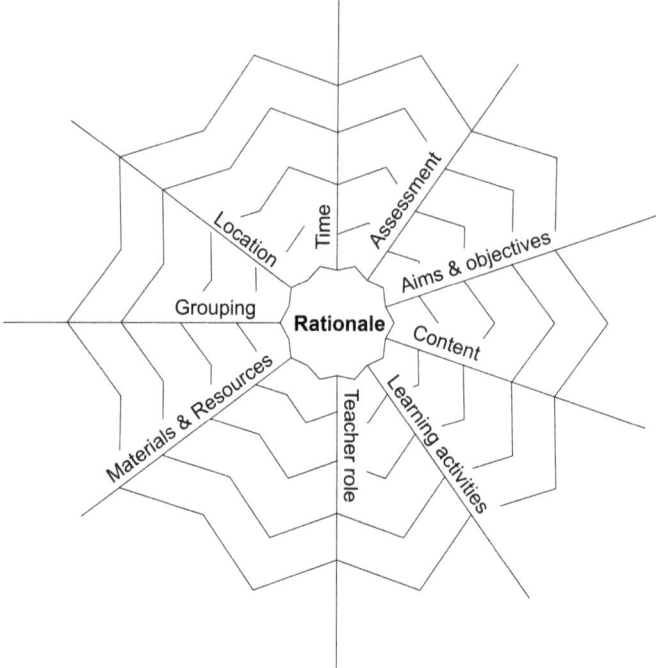

Fig. 3.1 The curricular spider web (retrieved from Van den Akker, 2003)

All of the above then leads to a fourth factor that comes into play, namely that **the curriculum can be organised at different levels**, which Priestley and colleagues (2021) categorise as:

- the supra level (transnational discourse about curriculum, formulated by organisations like the European Union and the Organisation for Economic Co-operation and Development (OECD);
- the macro level (national level on which curriculum frameworks and standards are developed such as the national curriculum in England;
- the meso level (local curriculum agencies, textbook publishers, and educational designers that bring the curriculum to the classroom);
- the micro level (schools and teachers who design educational programs and their lesson plans);
- the nano level (classroom level where teachers translate standards and their content into teaching activities that result in student learning).

The degree of autonomy teachers have in shaping the curriculum depends on the local context, ranging from strict governmental control with a prescriptive curriculum and textbooks, including high-stake centralised testing, towards the other end of the spectrum where individual teachers have complete freedom in what they want to teach, without any form of output control. Considering the context and the ratio-nale at the different levels, and taking into account the insights about the intended, implemented, attained, null and hidden curriculum, it can easily be concluded that implementing a curriculum is indeed complex and its content should be subjected to thorough societal debate.

Stein and colleagues (2007) schematically illustrate the complexities in measuring the actual 'impact' of a curriculum on learning outcomes, identifying several medi-ating factors that can influence its implementation in a dynamic model "in a series of temporal phases from the printed page (the written curriculum), to the teachers' plans for instruction (the intended curriculum), to the actual implementation of curricular-based tasks in the classroom (the enacted curriculum) (p. 321)" (see Fig. 3.2). For instance, teachers' translation of the written curriculum (e.g. textbooks) into curric-ular intentions acts as an important mediating factor in what is eventually taught to and finally learned by students. Teachers' experience with the enactment of the curriculum in the classroom will also shape and transform their future interactions with the translation from the written to the intended curriculum.[1]

While its implementation is clearly complex, different trends with regard to the role of knowledge in the curriculum can still be identified, as will be further examined in the following section.

3.2   Curriculum as a Pendulum

The role of knowledge in the curriculum can be metaphorically described as a pendulum oscillating between two extremes, from highly visible to virtually invis-ible knowledge elements. This pendulum swing is especially noticeable at the macro level. As discussed above, curriculum implementation is complex, which means that what happens at the macro level does not necessarily immediately occur in the class-room. Therefore, in what follows we will first discuss trends regarding the role of knowledge in the written curriculum rather than its full implementation in the class-room. Let us consider two examples of the written curriculum at the macro level to illustrate this point. In Fig. 3.3 you find an excerpt from the Belgian national history curriculum for primary education in 1954.

Imagine us asking a random Belgian student in 1960: "When and where was Napoleon defeated?" It is reasonable to assume that most students could answer this question. Knowledge items are prominent in this curriculum, ensuring that the awareness of these historical figures and events is not left to chance. Every Belgian

---

[1] This use of the term 'intended' differs from its use in the international assessment TIMSS, where 'intended' refers to what Stein et al. name 'written curriculum'.

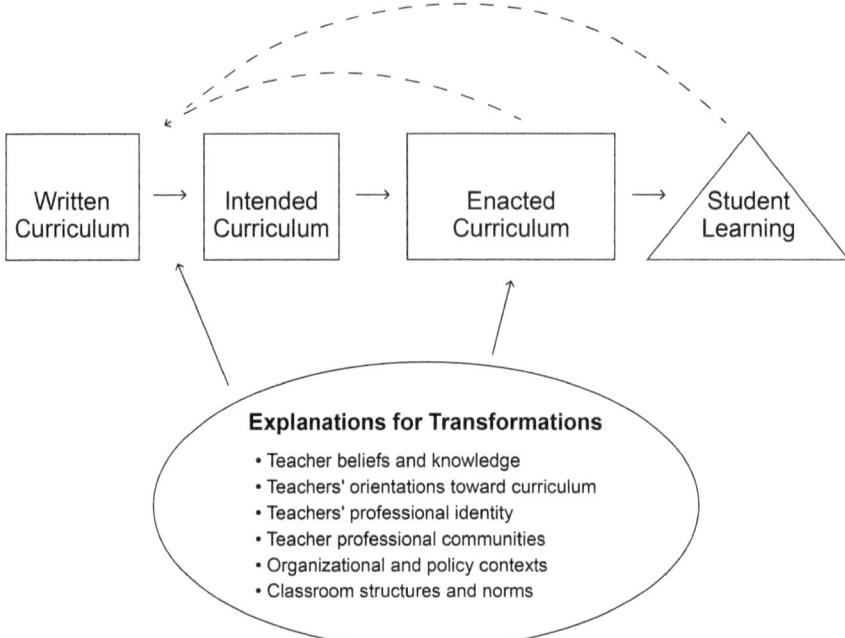

Fig. 3.2 Curriculum implementation (retrieved from Stein et al., 2007)

Students must know what happened at the following locations:

- Reims - Baptism of Clovis in 506.
- Poitiers - Victory of Charles Martel over the Moors.
- Aachen - Seat of the palace school and the tomb of Charlemagne.
- Verdun - Treaty of Verdun in 843. - Arrangement for the division of Charlemagne's empire.
- Jerusalem - Capital of the Holy Land. - Captured by the crusaders in 1099.
- Münster - Treaty of Westphalia in 1648 between Spain and the United Provinces of the Netherlands — Separation between the southern and northern provinces.
- Waterloo - Defeat of Napoleon in 1815.
- Yser - Halting the German advance in 1914.

They should also know what the following words and expressions mean:

Druid - Truce of God - Bruges - Matins - Charter - States General Mayfield - Belfry - Crafts and Guilds - Patrician - ...

Fig. 3.3 Snippet from 1954 Belgian national history curriculum for primary education (translated from Dutch)

child attending primary education at that time would likely have had some notions of Napoleon and Charlemagne. However, if we were to ask those same students how Napoleon's defeat was an indirect cause of the founding of the Belgian nation, the responses might vary. The question remains whether this is an issue. One could argue that the knowledge elements included here can act as future background knowledge to understand more complex curricular content in secondary education. When discussing 20th-century European history, history teachers know that all students should be familiar with Napoleon and Waterloo, making it easier to study historical texts and organise class discussions as there is some common ground on the topic. On the other hand, this curricular approach can be tempting to focus solely on the prescribed content knowledge, and thus limit oneself to rote learning. If the curricular goal was simply for students to memorise isolated facts, they could learn them in any order. After all, one isolated fact is as easy to learn as any other. Hence, we could compile a canonesque list (i.e. an authoritative and sanctioned collection of everything we want students to know), teach them in any random order, and tick off the list when it has been taught in the classroom. However, without connections between knowledge areas, it is guaranteed the understanding will be shallow, and retention will be poor. Let us now consider a second example of knowledge representation in the written curriculum at the macro level: an excerpt from the Welsh national science curriculum (Fig. 3.4).

This type of curriculum can be associated with 'the new curriculum' (Priestley & Sinnema, 2014), and can be closely tied to the societal influences and changes described in the previous part of this book. This contrast appears as a kind of pendulum movement whenever educational systems react against a more prescriptive curriculum at the macro level. Although its implementation varies from one country to another some commonalities can be identified.

Being curious and searching for answers is essential to understanding and predicting phenomena.

Progression step 1	Progression step 2	Progression step 3
I can show curiosity and question how things work. I can explore the environment, make observations and communicate my ideas.	I can ask questions and use my experience to suggest simple methods of inquiry. I can recognise patterns from my observations and investigations and can communicate my findings. I can use my knowledge and understanding to predict effects as part. (Gwybodaeth) Facts, information and skills acquired through experience or education; the theoretical or practical understanding of a discipline.	I can identify questions that can be investigated scientifically and suggest suitable methods of inquiry. I can suggest conclusions as a result of carrying out my inquiries. I can evaluate methods to suggest improvements.

Fig. 3.4 Welsh national science curriculum (retrieved from https://hwb.gov.wales/curriculum-for-wales)

First, the so-called new curriculum is mostly associated with **skill-oriented** standards that focus on generic competencies and 21st-century skills, often defined irrespective of specific content topics, and formulated as student outcomes (Meyer & Benavot, 2013). Generic competencies such as critical thinking, problem-solving, creative thinking, communicating, and entrepreneurship are often included. As previously mentioned, a substantial body of research has shown that these competencies cannot be taught independently of content.

Second, there can be **a lack of specificity** in terms of which knowledge should be acquired, posing challenges for school leaders, teachers, textbook makers, and test developers in interpreting the curriculum (Priestley & Sinnema, 2014). For instance, in 'being curious and searching for answers is essential to understanding and predicting phenomena', teachers might not know which 'phenomena' students have previously studied. A lack of clarity risks a lack of coherence, not only in terms of previously acquired knowledge and learning progressions within and across subjects, but also within other aspects of the educational system, such as (national) assessment, accountability, inspection, professional development, etc. (Oates, 2011). We will discuss this in more detail below. Also, broadly formulated standards at the macro level are often intended to grant more autonomy to teachers and schools. Nieveen and Kuiper (2021) highlight, however, that variation in the interpretation of standards in Dutch schools is so diverse that monitoring educational quality has become nearly impossible. Kuiper and Berkvens (2013) conclude that these standards do not automatically lead to autonomous decisions taken by teachers regarding the curriculum. This occurs for several reasons. For instance, school leadership teams and teachers may not always have sufficient expertise to handle this freedom, often relying heavily on textbooks. Or, experienced curricular freedom is constrained by strict output regulations, such as high-stakes national testing or rigorous inspection.

A third feature concerns the **learner-oriented pedagogies** implied by curricular goals such as 'explore and observe'. From this viewpoint, the curriculum focuses on the students' interests and experiences and differentiates to an individual level based on the students' needs. It also prescribes how teachers should enact the curriculum. It is not enough to learn about a topic; students should also 'experience' it, and 'reflect' on it. This is often accompanied by the concept of *learning to learn* and letting students become responsible for their own learning (Sinnema & Aitken, 2013).

A fourth feature we can distinguish is the tendency to strive for **over-ambitious thinking targets too early** in education, and independent of the required background knowledge, such as teaching generic 'problem-solving' in early childhood education (Britz, 1993), or 'thinking scientifically' with three-to five-year-olds in Wales. Of course there is nothing wrong with conceptual thinking at a young age. Children should learn abstract ideas like, for instance, the meaning of the equal sign. At the same time we also know from the first part of this book that children are not (yet) 'mini-historians' or 'mini-scientists', precisely because they still need to build sufficient knowledge schemas to handle those complex cognitive thinking skills

(Kirschner & Hendrick, 2020). It is important to build those necessary foundations before you can move on to complex thinking skills within a domain.

The two curriculum examples discussed above highlight distinct approaches to incorporating knowledge into the written curriculum at the macro level. In the first instance, knowledge takes a prominent role at the core of the curriculum, yet in a static fashion with a list of things every child should know, without encouraging any further interaction with the material. We know, however, that in order to facilitate background knowledge that truly supports future learning and reading, it is important to build true knowledge networks with coherent clusters of concepts in a domain (Neuman et al., 2014). Conversely, the second example portrays a contrasting extreme where knowledge seems rather absent, focusing on interactive engagement to gain generic competencies. As previously mentioned, there is of course a difference between the written and enacted curriculum. Having this type of written curriculum does not automatically mean that, for instance, tick box behavior will take place, but it might have a subtle influence.

Both examples can be positioned in Young and Muller's (2010) perspectives of thinking about curriculum, which they labelled as 'futures'. The first example touches upon a so-called *Future 1 curriculum,* what can be described as a collection of learning content, treating knowledge as fixed, unchanging and based on tradition. These curriculum types typically organise content into traditional subjects and can be traced back to the schooling system that established a formal curriculum of essential knowledge in the 19th and early twentieth centuries. In their extremest forms they could be described as absolute scripts for ingestion. The second example, on the other hand, touches upon a so-called *Future 2* curriculum and can be associated with the societal changes described in the previous part of this book. It holds a radical constructivist view of knowledge, a learner-oriented focus, and prioritises an outcome-based curriculum that reduces knowledge's central role in further learning, and in developing complex skills in school. It is important to point out, however, that re-embracing the importance of knowledge does not imply advocating a Future 1-curriculum, as both futures have their challenges. Yet, as noted by Muller (2023), the historical shift from Future 1 to Future 2-curriculum involved the elimination of both the negative ánd the positive elements of Future 1, which is why a return to knowledge must consider the lessons learned from this pendulum movement.

3.3   Towards the Best of Both Worlds: A Knowledge-Rich Curriculum

> In training a child to activity of thought, above all things we must beware of what I will call 'inert ideas'—that is to say, ideas that are merely received into the mind without being utilised, or tested, or thrown into fresh combinations. (Whitehead, 1929, p.1)

In this third section, we focus on a curriculum designed to address the challenges posed by the pendulum movement as described above, which we henceforth refer to as a **knowledge-rich curriculum.** Our rationale is clear: given the importance of knowledge for further learning, as a prerequisite for teaching complex skills in school, and from a democratic and emancipatory perspective, it should have a central and visible place in the curriculum. At the same time, this does not imply that the curriculum should just provide a list of concepts and facts students should know, and teachers should be reduced to mere transmitters of knowledge. Neither does it imply that a knowledge-rich curriculum is built by cherry picking some knowledge elements from one curriculum and adding a few important skills from another in an eclectic way, aiming for the middle ground between both extremes, such as the pendulum metaphor may wrongfully suggest. It cannot be overstated that we aim for deep and meaningful learning, both deep understanding and application of concepts, and therefore do not overlook the importance of complex thinking skills (such as problem-solving, critical thinking and reading comprehension), as they are crucial aspects to real understanding. These skills are, however, developed as students develop knowledge in a deep way. On the one hand, skills are a byproduct of domain-specific knowledge. On the other, they are better developed when teaching is also skill-concerned and focused on the correct interpretation and application of knowledge. In other words, in designing and implementing the curriculum, it is important to have a knowledge-led approach (Crato, 2025). Yes, we are greedy. We want it all.

Returning to the provisional definition of curriculum in the first section, we can hereby specify that a knowledge-rich curriculum is defined as follows:

> a plan for learning over time that is concept-led and knowledge-led (Oates, 2011), which encompasses a wide range of specified knowledge, and provides ample depth and opportunities to engage with that knowledge (Rata, 2021a). It sets high expectations for all students and systematically builds their knowledge of words and the world (Hirsch, 2016). It aims at a broad and steady foundation for complex thinking skills, such as critical thinking and reading comprehension, but also knowledge building that is further amplified and deepened by those complex skills. A comprehensive knowledge-rich curriculum covers subjects and concepts that go beyond children's day-to-day experiences and is based on the 'best' disciplinary knowledge available at that time (Young & Lambert, 2014). It ensures that every child has access to a broad and solid knowledge base in school, even if it has not been (partially) acquired from an early age onwards outside school.

However, building a knowledge-rich curriculum is not an easy task. Different authors will have their own perspectives on the key principles of a knowledge-rich curriculum. Although a comprehensive list of principles may be more inclusive, it can also become unwieldy. A brief list may miss out on crucial aspects, yet it can still serve as a useful outline. Therefore, we present three overarching principles that we found to be most beneficial and influential in understanding how a knowledge-rich curriculum can enhance learning, namely (1) content-richness, (2) coherence, and (3) clarity.

3.4 On Content-Richness

A curriculum led by concepts and knowledge might initially seem clear and straight-forward. It is not. A number of crucial questions come to the fore quickly, demanding thorough and deep analysis. Which content and concepts should be selected? What knowledge cannot be left to chance? And who decides? The answers to those questions will strongly depend on the purpose and context of the educational system and the specific level at which curriculum is being built. Therefore, a societal debate represented by the stakeholders in education is of utmost importance and must be thoroughly held. It also implies that socio-political factors will influence the answers (Thijs & van den Akker, 2009). In what follows, we aim to provide some guidelines as to (a) which content to select; (b) on what basis choices can be made; (c) how hierarchy and structure in knowledge have an impact on sequence; and (d) how to balance knowledge and skills.

3.4.1 The Selection of Content

First, which content do we want students to learn in school? Recent 'back-to-basics' movements have advocated allocating more time to mathematics and first language instruction in primary education. However, additional disciplines from the humanities, arts, and sciences can provide a broader perspective on the world and equip students with the comprehensive knowledge base necessary for acquiring and executing complex cognitive skills such as reading comprehension. But not only that. A healthy and balanced curriculum is needed for students to find their "element", that is, what they are passionate about and good at. Hence, a diverse range of subjects and experiences is necessary, thus including traditional academic disciplines as well as creative arts, technology, and other areas of study (Wiliam, 2013).

An important issue, however, is time. Every curriculum committee is tasked with reducing the coverage and yet everyone increases it. There indeed is a tendency to incorporate every societal issue in education, while the educational system cannot tackle, let alone solve, every societal concern (Cuban, 1992, as cited by van den Akker et al., 2003). As Whitehead noted in 1929: "We enunciate two educational commandments, 'Do not teach too many subjects,' and again, 'What you teach, teach thoroughly. (p. 2)" The risk of overload is legitimate and forces us to make choices between what we consider important and even more important (Wiliam, 2013), and this inevitably means that some content will not be part of the curriculum (*the null curriculum*; Eisner, 1985). Educational programs in high-performing countries also seem to focus on fewer topics but emphasise teaching them in a deeper and more profound manner (Schmidt et al., 2002). We should therefore avoid a curriculum that is "a mile wide and an inch deep" (Schmidt, McKnight & Raizen, 1997, p. 62). A guiding question on this matter could be: What should not be left to chance? This is not to say that we should restrict the curriculum entirely to just a few important disciplines or subjects. Knowledge and concepts are not limited to disciplinary boundaries. Tackling a topic or concept from different disciplines and viewpoints allows digging deeper into it, broadening knowledge schemas in long-term memory, and, if the topics are well-chosen, provide a broad yet sufficiently profound knowledge base for all students.

These insights regarding the selection and specificity of content also prompt the question of at what level these choices should be made, and to what degree. From a democratic perspective, with a view to creating a common knowledge base one could argue to determine and specify most of the content at the macro level. However, it is also important to consider the highly diverse contexts of different schools within an education system and to be mindful of their local context. This can naturally only be achieved by also providing certain degrees of freedom and autonomy, allowing schools and teachers to shape the curriculum. A fully prescriptive curriculum at the macro level that aims to select and specify a hundred percent of the lesson time would of course jeopardize the crucial role schools and teachers play in the context-specific enactment of the curriculum. However, as Oates (2011) points out, a certain degree of curricular control is equally necessary, as it also contributes to the coherence within an education system. We will further elaborate on this point below. On what basis can choices be made?

3.4.2 The Basis of the Selection Process

For this second aspect regarding content selection, it is useful to look at the knowledge theories of social realists, who advocate a revaluation of the role of **disciplinary knowledge** in education, which they differentiate from *everyday* knowledge. Whereas the latter arises from daily experiences and the social environment, much akin to what Geary (2012) calls 'folk-knowledge', disciplinary knowledge is built upon centuries of systematic study by specialist communities in areas such as mathematics, biology, physics, and more. For some disciplines, however, this is easier and more straightforward than for others. However, regarding the curriculum, let us keep it simple: disciplinary knowledge enables us to consider things that are unlikely to be known solely through experiences or observations. For instance, merely observing a polluted river will never allow us to comprehend the chemical element 'nitrogen'

(Rata, 2021a, 2021b). This is when disciplinary knowledge from chemistry is needed. By learning about this concept in a chemistry class, students can understand the effects of nitrates on land and waterways. In terms of reliability and objectivity, there is, therefore, more solid knowledge that can guide the curriculum and create a language to provide insight into a world beyond one's own current experiences or observations. A critical point, however, must be held in mind. While acknowledging that some knowledge is more solid and better grounded than others, it does not imply that knowledge is fixed. Consider our knowledge of dinosaurs. When the first Iguanodon was discovered, it was depicted with a horn on its nose (see Fig. 3.5). Meanwhile, we now know that this 'horn' was actually a claw, which was probably used in defence of predators (see Fig. 3.6). When contemplating curriculum, this is a principle that we must always keep in mind, emphasising the importance of structural curriculum revisions based on state-of-the-art disciplinary knowledge.

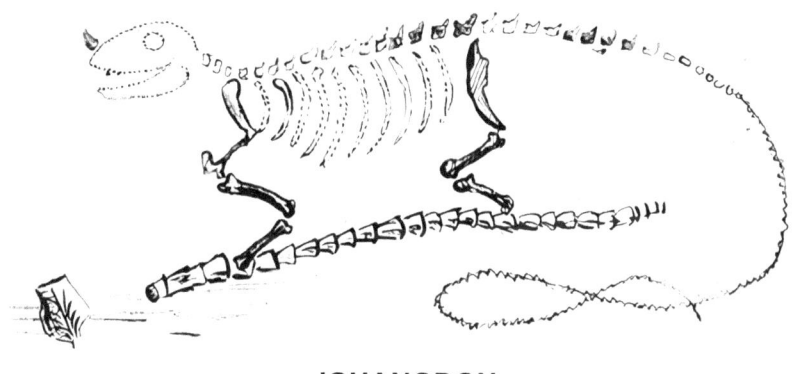

IGUANODON

Fig. 3.5 First drawing of an Iguanadon by Mantell (1834)

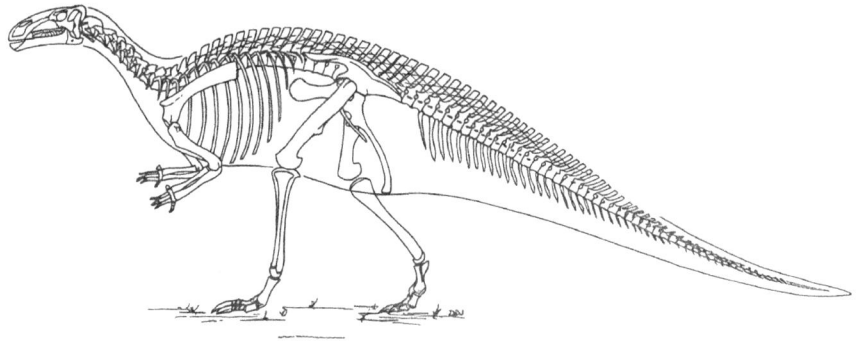

Fig. 3.6 Later drawing of an Iguanodon. Retrieved from Slate Weasel–Own work, CC BY-SA 4.0, https://commons.wikimedia.org/w/index.php?curid=97909961)

3.4.3 The Impact of Hierarchy and Structure in Knowledge and Sequence

A third aspect that is important to consider is the hierarchy and structure within the knowledge itself, and how this influences the careful sequencing of topics in the curriculum. For instance, when teaching about the impact of microplastics in water on the human body, numerous concepts must be grasped, including microplastics, water as a biotope and as a human resource, and the human body, including digestion. Each of these concepts can also be approached from various disciplines with their own disciplinary hierarchy. Content selection thus automatically puts curriculum makers in a position wherein a learning plan must be determined within and across disciplines. From a biological point of view, for example, it would be useful to determine what you need to know about the human body before you can come to a solid or necessary understanding of the human digestive system to tackle the microplastics problem. One must also take into consideration what was learned across disciplines to determine whether all necessary knowledge building blocks are in place to tackle the new problem. Below, we will discuss this further in the section on curriculum coherence. We want to emphasise here that if we consider 'the impact of microplastics on the body' to be part of the curriculum, prerequisite knowledge leading to understanding this concept must be included in the curriculum, starting in the earlier years. This aligns perfectly with the ideas posited by Ausubel (1968) on meaningful learning. When our goal is for students to engage with knowledge, hence providing them with meaningful learning activities, led by concepts and knowledge, we must take into consideration that the most important single factor influencing learning is what the learner already knows. It is important to note that content is not restricted by age, and knowledge building can start from a very young age. A thoughtful, content-rich early years curriculum can complement a nurturing, play-learning environment. Contrary to earlier beliefs about Piaget's developmental stages, the developmental processes in children are continuous and variable, with more variability than consistency in children's abilities (Willingham, 2008). Dispelling myths about preschool education, preschoolers are more knowledge-ready than commonly thought, and individual differences in exposure to knowledge strongly influence their development. As Bruner already hypothesised in 1960 (p. 33): "Each subject can be taught effectively in some intellectually honest form to any child at any stage of development".

3.4.4 The Relation Between Knowledge and Skills

"Content in the absence of thinking is inert and meaningless; but thinking in the absence of content is vacuous." (Robert. J. Sternberg, cited in Tobias and Duffy (2009, p. 10))

A fourth and very important aspect to discuss regarding content-selection in a knowledge-rich curriculum is the relation between knowledge and skills. This relation is often presented as a false dichotomy, suggesting that a focus on one would exclude a focus on the other, and vice versa. It seems useful to pause for a brief moment to consider what is meant by the term 'skills'. On the one hand, there are complex cognitive skills as discussed in the first section of this book, which mainly rely on domain-specific knowledge, and are hardly teachable in a generic way, outside a specific context. To be able to think critically about something and deeply understand a text on a particular topic, you need a solid base of background knowledge on that topic. Making sense of things and being able to apply it in novel situations is, in fact, memory in disguise. We also noted that there has been a shift in curricula over the past decades with a more explicit focus on skills, yet without sufficiently including the necessary knowledge base. However, we also emphasised that we do not advocate curricula that solely promote memorisation of disconnected facts. From our rationale and our understanding of the importance of knowledge, these complex skills do deserve a significant place in the curriculum, yet within specific domains, and with a view to deep understanding of specific concepts.

On the other hand, there are also more 'mechanical' skills that can be taught within a specific subject domain itself. Consider, for example, a program where students must learn welding. The basic act of welding is something to be practiced and automated before moving on to more complex situations. The same can be said for multiplication tables or solving addition problems. As pointed out earlier in this book, just like a professional footballer that may have endlessly practiced in isolation taking the perfect free kick to place the ball perfectly in the upper corner, certain skills can also be practiced and automated in the school context with a view to their application in more complex scenarios. Time to practice these skills is something that needs to be considered when selecting content in the curriculum, as well as how these skills evolve in complexity and context. A future stone mason who has only practiced using the same materials and the same tools in the same situation, will possibly encounter difficulties when those materials or tools are absent in new situations. Therefore, it can be helpful in a knowledge-rich curriculum, for students to understand the underlying rationale of certain techniques and even materials, enabling them to better assess new situations, selecting reasons for executing specific actions in a particular way, and approaching them creatively. While making mortar, based on knowledge, the future mason should be able to decide how much sand, cement, water and soap ought to be added to the mixture, whatever the weather conditions may be (i.e., when it rains the sand is wet, therefore less water is needed), instead of blindly following a fixed recipe (e.g., three parts sand, one part cement, one part water, a cup of soap).

The placement of these skills, however, will largely depend on the sequence in which concepts and knowledge are introduced. As mentioned above, the hierarchy and structure of knowledge concepts serve as an important guide in creating a coherent curriculum, with new knowledge building upon what was previously learned and increasing in complexity. For example, within a subject like physics, it would be logical to learn states of matter, gases, compressibility of gases, pressure, elasticity, and so on. A curriculum that is concept- and knowledge-led aims to incorporate important skills in this sequence, thus organising them in a logical manner based on the knowledge hierarchy at hand. This is in contrast to a curriculum where (generic) skills are central, risking a fragmented and episodic presentation of knowledge elements without considering their hierarchical structure and logical progression in complexity. For instance, let us consider the skill of fixing a flat tire. We can start from this skill to teach many of the earlier mentioned concepts in physics such as pressure, gases compressibility, elasticity … But to predominantly follow a skills-led approach runs the risk of not leading to a structured knowledge of physics, but to disconnected concepts. Looking back at the example from the written curriculum at the macro level in Wales, we can see this reflected as well. Although the importance of knowledge is not denied, no systematic structure respects its hierarchical nature. Attempts are made to describe an increase in complexity regarding the skills themselves, but it quickly becomes difficult to differentiate between simple methods of inquiry (progression step 2) and suitable methods of inquiry (progression step 3). In the section on clarity, we will further elaborate on this topic. Again, we want to emphasise that we by no means deny the importance of skills, and that they constitute an important part of the curriculum. Therefore, it is necessary to consider how the included knowledge will be applied when it comes to content selection.

3.5   On Coherence

Curriculum coherence is a precise technical term that not only entails arranging content in such an order that it supports age-related progression, but also aligns all components of the educational system in such a way that they are working together effectively to achieve educational objectives (Oates, 2011; Schmidt & Prawat, 2006). On the one hand, a coherent curriculum thus considers the organisation of the concepts and content within it and will be vital if one is to create a seamless and logical conceptual progression in what children learn over time, referred to by Thijs and van den Akker (2009) as vertical coherence. However, as stated above, knowledge and concepts are not limited to the boundaries of disciplines. It is therefore important to take into account how these concepts align with each other across subjects, which is referred to as horizontal coherence (Thijs & van den Akker, 2009). On the other hand, a coherent curriculum also implies alignment in terms of learning goals, pedagogy, teaching materials, etc. In the current section we will address vertical and horizontal coherence, namely the organisational structure within the curriculum and its content and concepts, followed by coherence and disciplinary knowledge. In the following section on *clarity*, we will discuss coherent system alignment in more detail.

3.5.1 Horizontal Coherence

Horizontal coherence refers to the organisation of content across topics, subjects, and domains, based on the idea that **subjects are not isolated bodies of knowledge**. When connections regarding concepts between different fields of study are not explicitly made, most students have difficulty making the connections themselves (Wiliam, 2013). Consider, for example, the concept of 'woman'. Would students gain a comprehensive understanding if they approach this concept solely from the field of biology? To grasp its full complexity, it would probably be necessary to explore how the role of women has evolved throughout history, how different religions perceive femininity and the place of the woman therein, and how social role patterns unfold in various societies and cultures around the world. Particularly in primary education, theme-based education can be a well-thought approach to facilitate deep learning about the same concept from various subject areas in the course of several weeks. However, it should be held in mind that disciplinary knowledge offers powerful ways of thinking about the world that does not develop naturally. Effective interdisciplinary work thus relies on solid disciplinary foundations and engagement (Rata, 2019; Wiliam, 2013). Moreover, when themes are developed without thinking about carefully sequencing the different topics and concepts in time knowledge building runs the risk of becoming fragmented. In contrast to a theme-based approach, the disciplinary approach treats concepts within the boundaries of the different disciplines. The disciplinary approach is often adopted in secondary schools, but can also be adopted earlier on, as shown below in the example of the Primary Knowledge Curriculum.

3.5.2 Vertical Coherence

> "It is in all cases more powerful to be concerned about connecting the lesson with prior learning and understanding than attend to the oft-made claims of relating the lessons to the real or some future world." (Hattie, 2023, p. 303)

Vertical coherence is about ensuring logical progression over time (weeks, months, years, and grades), where prior learning forms a foundation for future content. For instance, in preschool, teachers can already engage in knowledge-building activities, such as situating different countries on a globe (see Curriculum Case 1). When geographical concepts are systematically and sequentially expanded over the years, students develop the necessary schemas to address more complex and contemporary topics. Discussing, for instance, slavery in colonial history, or religious conflicts in the Middle East becomes less cognitively taxing when students already have a firm grasp of world regions, countries and capitals, of natural resources and their role in wealth creation, etc. A clearly sequenced curriculum provides teachers with a roadmap that guides them **from what is known to what has to be learned**. It is crucial to emphasise that we are discussing substantive sequence here, where we let the content guide the progression rather than achievement levels.

However, content sequencing is complex, demands careful consideration, and is seldom linear. Consider, for example, the sequence of teaching geometric shapes. In various European countries, it is common to teach triangles first, followed by parallelograms. In Japan, it is the other way around, as parallelograms consist of two triangles. Although there is no perfect universal sequence that applies to everyone, thinking about sequence helps determine what students need to know before moving on. Otherwise learning can become fragmented and episodic. For instance, one could teach about dinosaurs and the prehistoric ages in pre-school one week, and about Ancient Egypt during another. Although these lessons could be interesting and fun, valuable opportunities are missed to provide sufficient depth and a solid foundation for future learning, endangering the act of meaningful learning (Ausubel, 1968). In the same way as subjects require logical sequence based on prior knowledge, the timing of introducing and revisiting specific content is equally important. This principle is embodied in Jerome Bruner's *Spiral Curriculum* (1960), in which concepts are introduced early in the curriculum and revisited with increasing complexity.

Curriculum Case 1

Core Knowledge Foundation kindergarten curriculum

In the *Core Knowledge Curriculum* for kindergarten (Core Knowledge Foundation, 2010), knowledge is built and acquired cumulatively. Building upon foundations laid in earlier grades, learning about continents and oceans ('what students should already know'), kindergarteners are introduced to the voyages of Christopher Columbus, how he sailed to the American continent with the Niña, the Pinta, and the Santa María, and so on ('what students need to learn'). The following excerpt of the core curriculum illustrates how vertical coherence is implemented in practice by describing the prior knowledge kindergarteners should have acquired ('What Students Should Already Know') before systematically linking it to the new learning objectives ('What Students Need to Learn').

What Students Should Already Know

- What maps and globes represent and how they are used
- Rivers, lakes, and mountains: what they are and how they are represented on maps and globes
- The locations of the Atlantic Ocean and Pacific Ocean
- The locations of the North Pole and South Pole
- The meaning of some basic terms of spatial orientation necessary for working with maps
- The names and relative locations of the seven continents

- Some familiar associations with each continent, such as wildlife, landmarks, etc.
- The cultures of the Eastern Woodlands, American Southwest, and Pacific Northwest Native Americans, including how they lived, what they wore and ate, what their homes were like, what their beliefs and stories were/are, and what their status is today

What Students Need to Learn

The Voyage of Columbus in 1492

- How Queen Isabella and King Ferdinand funded Columbus's voyage
- The *Niña, Pinta*, and *Santa María*
- Why Columbus used the terms *Indies* and *Indians*
- Why Europeans thought Columbus had found a new world

The Pilgrims

- Why the Pilgrims founded a colony
- The *Mayflower* and Plymouth
- How the Thanksgiving Day celebration came about

July 4, Independence Day

- The birthday of the United States of America
- Democracy (rule of the people): Americans wanted to rule themselves rather than be governed by a faraway king
- Why freedom did not exist for all people in the new nation: some people were enslaved

3.5.3   Coherence and Disciplinary Knowledge

Moreover, coherence is also important at the level of disciplinary knowledge. In creating a curriculum, we must consider the structure of the knowledge itself. Coherent content standards in curriculum are organised as a logical sequence of topics, aligning with the hierarchical nature of disciplinary knowledge, ensuring that what and how students are taught reflects fundamental concepts within the academic discipline (Rata, 2021a; Schmidt et al., 2002). This reasoning is connected to the concept of 'big ideas', statements that attempt to describe some major understanding in a particular discipline, analogous to a giant mental schema with interconnected concepts. Big ideas can be used as a starting point to structure the curriculum, and the ideas themselves can be broken down into several important components, such as what needs to be assessed, what evidence is needed to determine whether students really understand certain concepts, and what students need to be able to know and do (Hattie, 2023; McTighe, 2000; Wiggins & McTighe, 2005; Wiliam, 2013). This helps us to see how the different topics are connected and allows us to see the coherence of the whole curriculum.

Curriculum Case 2

Big ideas of science–Retrieved from Wiliam (2013)

An international team of science education experts compiled a list of ten big ideas of science and an additional four fundamental ideas about science (Harlen et al., 2010).

- All material in the universe is made of very small particles.
- Objects can affect other objects at a distance.
- Changing the movement of an object requires a net force acting on it.
- The total amount of energy in the universe is always the same but energy can be transformed when things change or are made to happen.
- The composition of the Earth and its atmosphere and the processes occurring within them shape the earth's climate.
- The solar system is a very small part of one of millions of galaxies in the universe.
- Organisms are organised on a cellular basis.
- Organisms require a supply of energy and materials for which they are often dependent on or in competition with other organisms.
- Genetic information is passed from one generation of organisms to another.
- The diversity of organisms, living and extinct, is the result of evolution.

Big ideas about science

- Science assumes that for every effect there is one or more causes.
- Scientific explanations, theories and models are those that best fit the facts known at a particular time.
- The knowledge produced by science is used in some technologies to create products to serve human ends.
- Applications of science often have ethical, social, economic and political implications.

The concept of 'big ideas' is also illustrated in the *Curriculum Design Coherence Model* (CDC Model; Rata, 2019), where researchers, in collaboration with teachers, took disciplinary knowledge as a starting point in curriculum design (Rata, 2021a). The *Knowledge in Education Research Unit*, based at the University of Auckland in New Zealand, developed the CDC model. Since its creation in 2018, the CDC Model has undergone continuous development and is based on extensive research (Rata, 2021a). The model consists of four interconnected elements (see Fig. 3.7), with the first two elements relying on an understanding of different types of knowledge ('knowledge-that', a broad term used for the coherent connection of concepts and content. The third element is 'know-how-to', a term referring to skills in using the 'knowledge-that'). The CDC Model's purpose is to connect concepts, content, and the application thereof so they can be utilised to promote curriculum clarity and coherence. "The findings from the Knowledge Project indicate that […] using the CDC Model's concept-cohering approach to curriculum design provided a way to avoid the limitations of both content-list and skills-based approaches" (Rata, 2021a, p. 448).

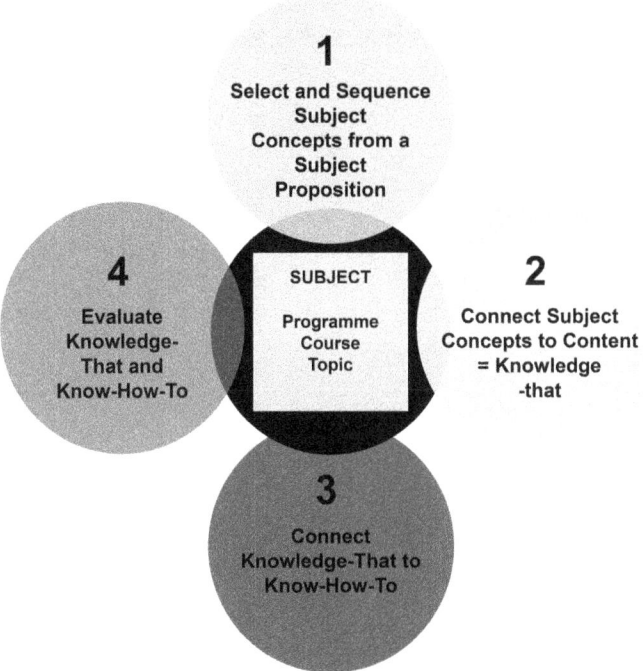

Fig. 3.7 The curriculum design coherence model (Rata, 2021a, 2021b)

Curriculum Case 3

*The CDC Model into practice (*Rata, 2021a, 2021b*)*

The CDC Model illustrates how the various principles of Content, Clarity, and Coherence are intricately connected. Below, the different steps are briefly outlined and illustrated.

Element 1: Selecting and sequencing subject concepts from a subject proposition

Teachers are required to outline a subject proposition and select the subject concepts. An example proposition on 'Exercise' in physical education: is 'Exercise utilises the body's *energy* to build *stamina* and *strength*' (concepts are italicised). This proposition links the subject to key concepts, providing coherence to the design process. Subject concepts are crucial for design coherence and remain consistent, but their meaning deepens in complexity over the years.

Element 2: Connecting subject concepts to content knowledge

The subject concepts identified in Element 1 are linked to actual course content, creating knowledge-that. This involves a back-and-forth process between subject concepts and content to achieve the best alignment. In the example of physical education, content expressing the 'strength' concept could include specific muscles' names, roles, and position. Subject content is not just an information list; it is a thoughtfully curated selection of material expressing the meaning of subject concepts. Three criteria were proposed for selection:

- Material should be selected based on quality and aims to express the proposition in a truthful manner.
- The fallible nature of knowledge should be acknowledged. New insights can emerge in various ways. Therefore, it can be useful to spend some time to include the intellectual history of the big idea or proposition from a particular discipline.
- Content selection is intentionally social and/or political. It is guided by the question: Is this the subject content that we, as a society, want the next generation of citizens to know?

Element 3: Connecting 'knowledge-that' to 'know-how-to'

This is the connection between 'knowledge-that' and 'know-how-to'. It encompasses two types of know-how-to: First, performance focuses on applying procedural rules in practice and achieving mastery. Second, judgment focuses on understanding subject concepts to solve problems and evaluate solutions through conceptual reasoning. Both need to be specifically taught and increase in complexity.

Element 4: Evaluating 'knowledge-that' and 'know-how-to'

The evaluation system is intended to assess how well students master know-how-to in relation to their understanding of 'knowledge-that'—the concept and substantive knowledge. Assessment and feedback are viewed in terms of:

- Recall: how well do learners remember the content?
- Skill and technique: how well can learners perform a certain skill or technique?
- Judgement know-how-to: how effectively can substantive knowledge be used to explain and justify the purpose of a specific action?

For more examples and further explanations about how to use the CDC model in practice, see Rata (2023).

3.6 On Clarity

Besides content-richness and coherence, a third important aspect of a knowledge-rich curriculum is clarity. We will illustrate the importance of curricular clarity with an example. In a Flemish technology curriculum at the macro level, it is stated that students should be able to 'illustrate how technical systems are based on knowledge about material characteristics or natural phenomena.' This example highlights that while knowledge is seen as a prerequisite, it is not explicitly articulated but viewed in function of skills. While this standard might be perceived as providing 'autonomy in implementation' to teachers, we previously noted that this freedom is often exercised by entities other than teachers themselves. Additionally, as shown earlier in the example from Wales, such objectives risk an incoherent curriculum, making it difficult to establish clear and systematic plans for learning. Furthermore, we also argued in the section on content selection that it is important to make choices regarding curriculum content and that a thorough debate is necessary. Although this debate is always social and political in nature, it is advisable to make clear decisions. However, in such a debate there is a risk in problematic consensus-seeking among different stakeholders, each aiming for their own content to be integrated. The result of this could be an amalgam of vague objectives where it becomes unclear what should and should not be included in the curriculum (Oates, 2011). Therefore, **setting clear expectations** is a third important characteristic of a knowledge-rich curriculum. We start this section by (a) emphasising the importance of clear goals for teachers and student learning. We then move on to the issue of (b) interpreting learning objectives and their impact on the discrepancy between the intended and the achieved curriculum. Finally, we address (c) the importance of good alignment in the educational system, including the curriculum, teaching, the teaching materials, assessment and quality monitoring, and other aspects of the system.

3.6.1 The Importance of Clear Learning Goals

The first aspect of curriculum clarity, the importance of clear learning goals, is rather straightforward: teachers should know what has previously been learned. If they know what students ought to know and be able to do at a specific age or grade level, teachers can effectively access and revisit existing prior knowledge before expanding on it. Remember the experiment with the sequence 106614921815 in the first part of this book? If knowledge and concepts are specified in the curriculum, the impact of prior knowledge on further learning becomes not just individual, but collective. Teachers can then draw upon a shared classroom foundation of prior knowledge rather than relying on the fragmented understanding of individual students, and frantically trying to provide that knowledge quickly to those who lack it.

It seems crucial to further explore at what curricular level clarity in learning goals should be organised to what extent. At the meso- and micro-levels, it is possible, and perhaps even logical, for teachers to build on what has previously been learned through clear objectives. However, the caveat that needs to be made here is that the societal impact also remains limited to the meso- and micro-level of the curriculum, namely the teachers, schools, or school groups that engage with it. If we revisit our rationale, where from a social-democratic perspective we aim to provide a common knowledge base, and give every child access to a robust knowledge foundation, the biggest impact can be achieved by setting clear expectations at the curricular macro level through clearly formulated goals. However, the level of specificity of these learning goals might differ between subjects, and distinct curricular levels in different educational systems. A shared understanding between educators is the goal, clarity is a means to this end.

3.6.2   The Interpretation of Learning Goals

A second aspect of curriculum clarity pertains to the interpretation of learning goals. As mentioned above, there is an ever-present discrepancy between what is *intended* at the curricular macro-level, and the *enacted* curriculum in classrooms (Bauersfeld, 1979; Thijs & van den Akker, 2009). The teacher is the key mediating factor in this translation process, deciding how the written curriculum turns into learning experiences and, ultimately, the knowledge and skills learned by students. Returning to our earlier example from the technology curriculum, 'to illustrate how technical systems are based on knowledge about material characteristics or natural phenomena', it is apparent that the possibilities to achieve this standard are boundless. For instance, while one teacher might be engaging 6-year olds in crafting festive Christmas hats from paper and cardboard, another might be introducing the principles of levers. The broader the standards, the more diverse the interpretations, transforming education into a lottery for students and parents regarding the depth and breadth of knowledge and skills provided at distinct schools. From a democratic and social perspective, it can even be argued that too broadly formulated learning goals jeopardise a shared and coherent knowledge base, which introduces the possibility of increasing knowledge inequality, and is most detrimental for disadvantaged students.

At the other end of the spectrum, an interesting example of integrating specific knowledge elements in the curriculum, while maintaining some degrees of freedom can be found in the following excerpt from the new English national curriculum, as shown in Fig. 3.8.

While some content in this example is very specific, such as naming and locating the world's seven continents and five oceans, others are more open to interpretation, like 'understanding geographical similarities and differences through studying the human and physical geography of a small area of the United Kingdom and a contrasting non-European country'. This provision enables geography teachers to weave in local, contextual nuances when translating the intended curriculum into practice. Concurrently, it establishes 'non-negotiables', namely a shared and specific understanding of fundamental geographical facts and figures as important building blocks for complex thinking skills within the geography domain.

Key stage 1

Pupils should develop knowledge about the world, the United Kingdom and their locality.

They should understand basic subject-specific vocabulary relating to human and physical geography and begin to use geographical skills, including first-hand observation, to enhance their locational awareness.

Pupils should be taught to:

Locational knowledge

- name and locate the world's seven continents and five oceans
- name, locate and identify characteristics of the four countries and capital cities of the United Kingdom and its surrounding seas

Place knowledge

- understand geographical similarities and differences through studying the human and physical geography of a small area of the United Kingdom, and of a small area in a contrasting non-European country

Human and physical geography

- identify seasonal and daily weather patterns in the United Kingdom and the location of hot and cold areas of the world in relation to the Equator and the North and South Poles

Fig. 3.8 English national curriculum (retrieved from https://assets.publishing.service.gov.uk/media/5a7c1ecae5274a1f5cc75e97/PRIMARY_national_curriculum_-_Geography.pdf)

Key stage 2

Pupils should extend their knowledge and understanding beyond the local area to include the United Kingdom and Europe, North and South America.

This will include the location and characteristics of a range of the world's most significant human and physical features. They should develop their use of geographical knowledge, understanding and skills to enhance their locational and place knowledge.

Pupils should be taught to:

Locational knowledge

• locate the world's countries, using maps to focus on Europe (including the location of Russia) and North and South America, concentrating on their environmental regions, key physical and human characteristics, countries, and major cities

• name and locate counties and cities of the United Kingdom, geographical regions and their identifying human and physical characteristics, key topographical features (including hills, mountains, coasts and rivers), and land-use patterns; and understand how some of these aspects have changed over time

• identify the position and significance of latitude, longitude, Equator, Northern Hemisphere, Southern Hemisphere, the Tropics of Cancer and Capricorn, Arctic and Antarctic Circle, the Prime/Greenwich Meridian and time zones (including day and night)

Fig. 3.8 (continued)

3.6.3   The Importance of Good Alignment

A third aspect regarding clarity, constitutes its impact on the alignment within the system. First, the discrepancy between the *intended* and the *achieved curriculum* will eventually depend on the teachers' quality and the materials used. In some countries, such as the UK, teachers seem to create many learning materials themselves (Oates, 2014). While this may appear positive at a first glance, there are risks. Apart from the impact on workload, it may also lead to a lack of coherence and clear learning progressions (Steiner et al., 2018). On the other hand, in many countries teachers mainly rely upon textbooks, which seem to play a crucial role in improving educational systems and in supporting effective teaching and learning (Oates, 2014). However, the quality of these materials can vary significantly, directly affecting learning outcomes and student achievement (Dockx et al., 2020), especially where commercial, rather than educational, interests dominate textbook design. If we combine these insights with the previous aspect, namely the interpretation of learning objectives, we also see that in many systems where teachers tend to rely heavily on textbooks, the interpretation of learning goals is mostly left to textbook makers. Although some systems have quality control in place, others do not, and thus the interpretation of learning objectives depends more on commercial players. Therefore, clear learning goals at the macro and meso level have the potential to minimise a variety of interpretations, hence minimising the discrepancy and assuring better alignment between the intended, the enacted and the achieved curriculum.

Second, clarity in goals can not only lead to better alignment between the learning goals and activities. Clarity also means that we can more reliably assess to what extent these learning goals have actually been achieved. Consider, for instance, the contrast between the following three intentions made at the beginning of the new year:

- I aspire to engage in more athletic activities in 2024.
- I have set my sights on increasing my running routine in 2024.
- I am determined to complete a marathon in November 2024 in less than three hours.

While each of these intentions allows for a spectrum of interpretations and implementations, it is evident that the alignment and assessment of the last intention far surpasses its predecessors. If learning goals are not stated clearly, they result in a kaleidoscope of implementations while complicating the task of monitoring its quality (Steiner et al., 2018). At the macro level, especially in countries where some form of output regulation is organised through, for example, centralised testing or inspection, clear expectations can lead to better alignment between the intended and achieved curriculum and thus to better quality monitoring of the system itself. Interestingly, Oates (2011) and Wiliam (2014) elaborate on this interaction between curriculum and assessment at the macro level, and list several implications when this interaction is poor. Regarding clarity, Oates (2011) suggests that when statements are over-generic it will become difficult to develop fair tests due to the diversity in learning programmes. Thus, validity will be compromised. This leads, perhaps unexpectedly, to a form of teaching to the test in which "teachers have little choice under such circumstances to do anything other than relate learning to past test papers rather than the objectives of the curriculum, since the curriculum offers inadequate guidance as to what will appear in the tests (Oates, 2011, p. 131)".

While all of the above clearly points to the importance of clear learning objectives, at the same time some caution is warranted. Specificity implies several risks, one of which is the risk of curricular overload. Too many clear objectives could potentially lead to a perverse effect where those clear goals are reduced to a checklist and curriculum coverage instead of aiming for deeper understanding and true engagement with knowledge. It could also lead to overassessment, resulting in either excessively long tests, or tests that inadequately sample the domain, making it difficult to accurately measure students' achievements (Oates, 2011; Wiggins & McTighe, 2005). An additional caveat is that increasing specificity is not easy to do. McTighe (2000, p. 2) termed this the "Goldilocks problem": some learning goals are too big, some are too small and only a few are just right. In response to this problem, Wiggins and McTighe (2005) suggest identifying the "Big Ideas" and curriculum priorities based on the content, as illustrated in Fig. 3.9.

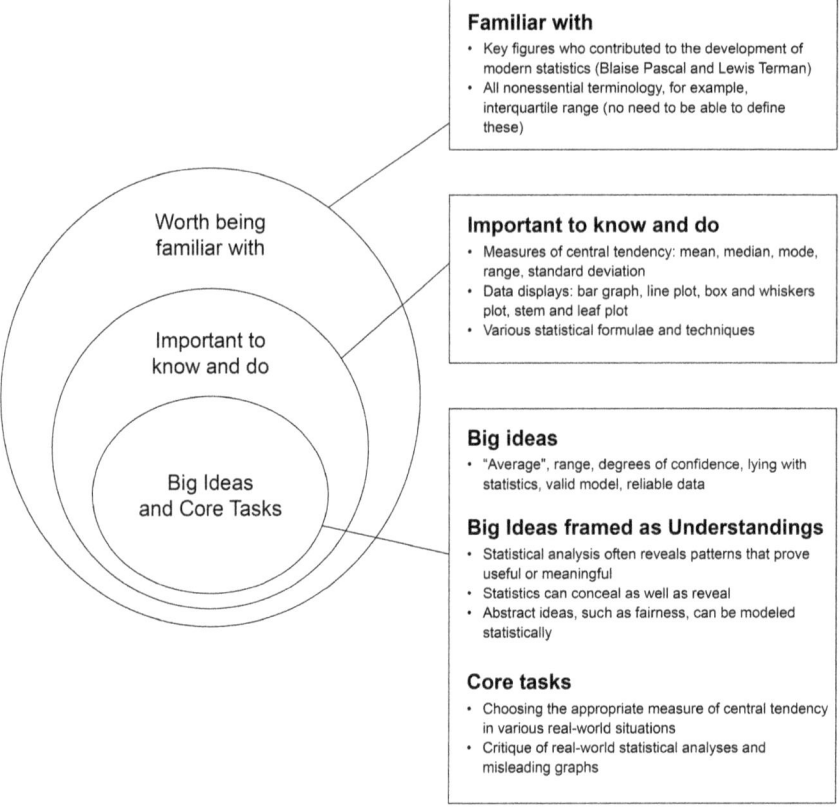

Familiar with
- Key figures who contributed to the development of modern statistics (Blaise Pascal and Lewis Terman)
- All nonessential terminology, for example, interquartile range (no need to be able to define these)

Important to know and do
- Measures of central tendency: mean, median, mode, range, standard deviation
- Data displays: bar graph, line plot, box and whiskers plot, stem and leaf plot
- Various statistical formulae and techniques

Big ideas
- "Average", range, degrees of confidence, lying with statistics, valid model, reliable data

Big Ideas framed as Understandings
- Statistical analysis often reveals patterns that prove useful or meaningful
- Statistics can conceal as well as reveal
- Abstract ideas, such as fairness, can be modeled statistically

Core tasks
- Choosing the appropriate measure of central tendency in various real-world situations
- Critique of real-world statistical analyses and misleading graphs

Fig. 3.9   Big ideas. Retrieved from Wiggins and McTighe (2005, p.71)

A third factor regarding system alignment is the **potential impact** of curriculum clarity **on other aspects of education**. If we expect kindergarten students to be introduced to concepts such as plate tectonics and volcanoes, it is evident that teachers delivering these contents should also have sufficiently mastered them (i.e., you cannot teach what you do not know; Kirschner et al., 2022). In an environment where clear concepts and knowledge lead the curriculum design, it is essential for teachers to learn about it in initial teacher education or even earlier and refine their expertise to align with evolving curriculum expectations. The curriculum therefore influences what should be learned in teacher education and professional development. This line of thinking might stir some debate in countries where teacher autonomy is cherished. However, Priestley and colleagues (2021, p. 2) argue that "teachers will always find ways to work around even the most prescriptive policies," and that experienced teachers were even more effective in doing so. Even with a specified and clear curriculum, teachers still shape the enacted curriculum (Watkins, 1997). A curriculum is transformed when it enters the classroom (Sizer, 1999; Stein et al., 2007); therefore, teacher quality remains of the highest importance, even when implementing the clearest curriculum.

Curriculum Case 4

Content, coherence and clarity into practice: The Primary Knowledge Curriculum

The Primary Knowledge Curriculum (PKC) has grown out of the Knowledge Schools Trust, a group of seven schools in London and Berkshire. Since 2013, driven by the idea of academic excellence and the desire to succeed for all children regardless of their background, this school group has been developing and enacting a knowledge-rich curriculum for its primary schools. To date, the Knowledge Schools Trusts has already worked with hundreds of schools and trusts nationwide in various contexts and supported them in embedding this curriculum in combination with high-quality professional development. The PKC is characterised by ambitious content that is well-specified and well-sequenced, horizontally as well as vertically. In what follows we will show how the three c's (content, coherence and clarity), as described above, can be put into practice.

Content-richness. The Primary Knowledge Curriculum is based on the idea of powerful knowledge. Its aim is for children to acquire knowledge that takes them beyond their everyday experiences through the knowledge and traditions of various disciplines. Looking at concepts through the lens of different disciplines, each having their own traditions and unique way of looking at the world, provides the opportunity to develop a deep understanding. For instance, while learning about Chinese painting in year 5 arts lessons children also learn about the Ming dynasty. In the example below, this is illustrated with the concept of 'trade', a concept that is tackled through history, geography and even arts.

Coherence. As previously stated, concepts are taught and learned in depth using knowledge from various disciplines. In contrast to thematic approaches, where the boundaries between disciplines sometimes blur, the PKC places importance on the distinct disciplines themselves, given the specific traditions that make each of these approaches unique. Crucial importance is also attached to vertical coherence, not only within but also across disciplines: In order being able to learn about globalisation in year 6 the foundations for the concept of "trade" are already put in place in the early years. In year 2, for instance, children learn in history lessons about ancient Romans in Britain and that forums functioned as marketplaces (as shown in Fig. 3.10). In year 3, from a geographical perspective, children learned that rivers are used by people to trade and that major cities developed alongside them. Furthermore, they learn that trade is the buying and selling of goods and services, and that many goods and services are being traded in Western Europe. From a historical perspective, children learn that unique skills and their products become valuable trade items in lessons about the Neolithic Age and about the link between migration and the exchange of goods, ideas, and technologies when encountering the Anglo-Saxons, Scots, and Vikings. As Fig. 3.10 shows, clear learning paths are designed, leaving very little to chance.

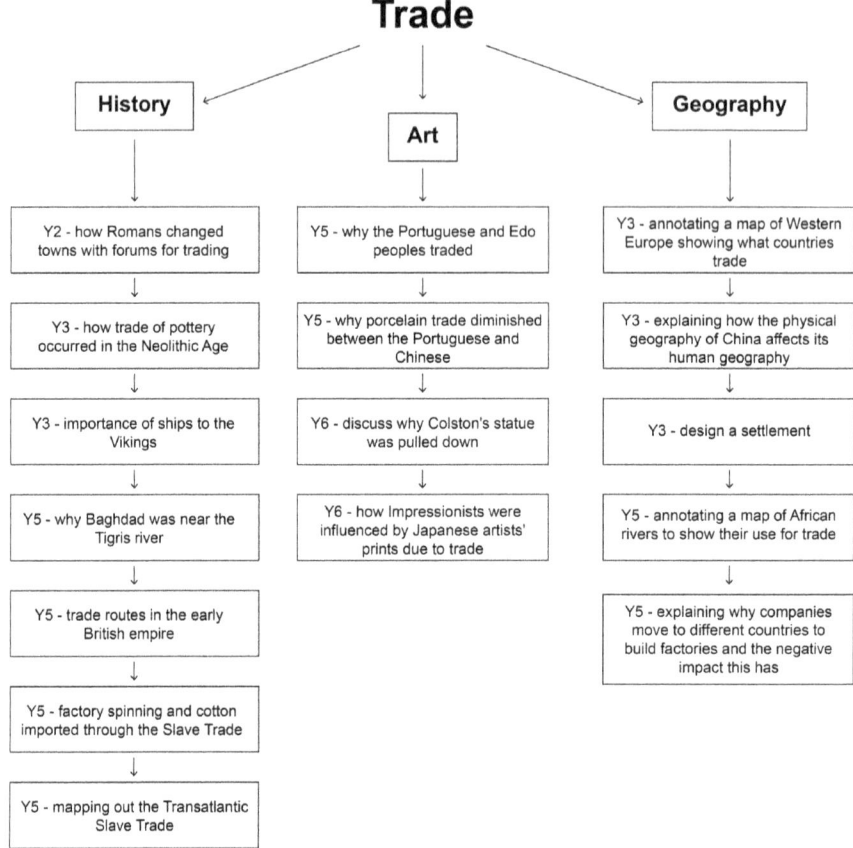

Fig. 3.10 Theme based curriculum building through disciplinary knowledge sequencing. *source* Primary Knowledge Curriculum

Clarity. The PKC is furthermore characterised by specifying the content to be learned. As illustrated by Fig. 3.11, learning objectives are formulated as big ideas that year 3 students need to capture as well as key vocabulary they need to master. Through specification of content, it becomes possible for teachers to purposely identify prior learning and then to build upon it.

Complex skills. By systematically building a solid foundation of knowledge and vocabulary within and across disciplinary domains, children become capable of undertaking complex activities, such as writing nuanced essays in which they address complex research questions like "how has globalisation changed the world." This is illustrated in the following example by a year 6 student (Fig. 3.12). These tasks not only allow students to demonstrate their learning but also reinforce and deepen their understanding.

Teacher knowledge
Trade is the buying and selling of goods and services. Countries in Western Europe trade many different goods and services. For the purpose of this lesson, we will focus on the trade of goods that are relatively familiar to children in Year Three. France: grows wheat, sugar, apples, pears, cherries, sells wine, beef, cheese. Germany: sweets, cheese, pork, wheat, barley, potatoes, carrots. Switzerland: known for chocolate, expensive watches and clocks. Austria: wine, beef, pork and cheese. Belgium: Diamonds (not mined in Belgium but skilled cutters and dealers based in Antwerp), chocolate, barley, corn, potatoes. Luxembourg: steel machinery, food, chemicals, barley, oats, grapes for wine. The Netherlands: machines, electrical items, fuel, wheat, potatoes, tulips. Countries in Western Europe trade with each other and other countries in Europe. During this lesson, children are building a conceptual understanding of trade; the exchange of goods. Children don't necessarily need to remember the exact products that each country trades, but it's important that they recognize different countries produce products that can be traded with other countries. The link between climate and the goods countries produce will be also be built upon in subsequent units.

Knowledge Objective	Lesson Detail	Vocabulary
To know that trade means buying and selling goods.	**Prior learning:** Check children are familiar with a map of Western Europe and can identify some, if not all of the countries within this region, alongside some corresponding information such as capital cities, languages and flags. **Vocabulary:** introduce the word 'trade' and explain that it means buying and selling goods such as food, machines, computers, cars etc. If France sells cheese to England, they are trading. Countries that buy goods from other countries are importing them, bringing them into the country. That same country might sell goods to another, this is called exporting. Think of 'export' as having a part of the word 'exit' in it, which means leave. When a country exports goods, they leave the country to go somewhere else. Import etymology, from Latin importare 'bring in', from in - 'in' + portare 'carry'. Export etymology, from Latin exportare, from ex- 'out' portare 'carry'.	• Trade • buying • selling • goods • crops • import • export
Knowledge Goals		
Countries in Western Europe trade with each other. Countries in Western Europe make products and sell them to other countries. Countries in Western Europe buy products from other countries.	**Teach:** Countries in Western Europe make things and grow things to trade. Show images of crops, animals, machinery. Explain that the temperate climate allows countries in Western Europe to grow lots of plants as crops, including wheat, sugar, barley, fruit, and vegetables. Recap the vegetables grown in Germany from the previous lessons. Some countries are also known for particular kinds of foods e.g. France: cheese, Belgium: chocolate. Model, using children to hold different goods, how a product is made in one country and then exported to another country. Also model how one country buys a product from another and that product is imported **Talk task:** what is the difference between import and export? **Task:** Annotate a blank map of Western Europe with images of what the country trades. Give children a table with information about the goods each country trades (see resources at end of unit) **Partner teach/ Plenary:** What is trade? What is traded in Western Europe? Explain that if the UK didn't trade with other countries, there are many products we wouldn't have, e.g. bananas, oranges, pineapples. Many things we use, such as medicines, electronics, clothes are made in other countries and imported to the UK. **Step for Depth:** Why do countries trade?	
Suggested Resources	Table containing information about the goods traded in each country.	

Fig. 3.11 Detailed lesson plan of a knowledge-rich curriculum. *source* Primary Knowledge Curriculum (PKC)

In summary, the curriculum as a concept is complex in its conceptualisation and how it is built and enacted in our educational institutions. Over the years the role of knowledge in the curriculum has, like a pendulum, shifted between extremes. Taking into account what we know from both the first and second part of this book, we want the best of both worlds, what has been identified as a knowledge-rich curriculum. This involves three overarching principles that we found to be most beneficial in understanding how a knowledge-rich curriculum can enhance learning, namely (1) content-richness, (2) coherence, and (3) clarity. Now that we know what a knowledge-rich curriculum looks like and why it is important, we will take a closer look at what is currently known about a knowledge-rich curriculum and student achievement.

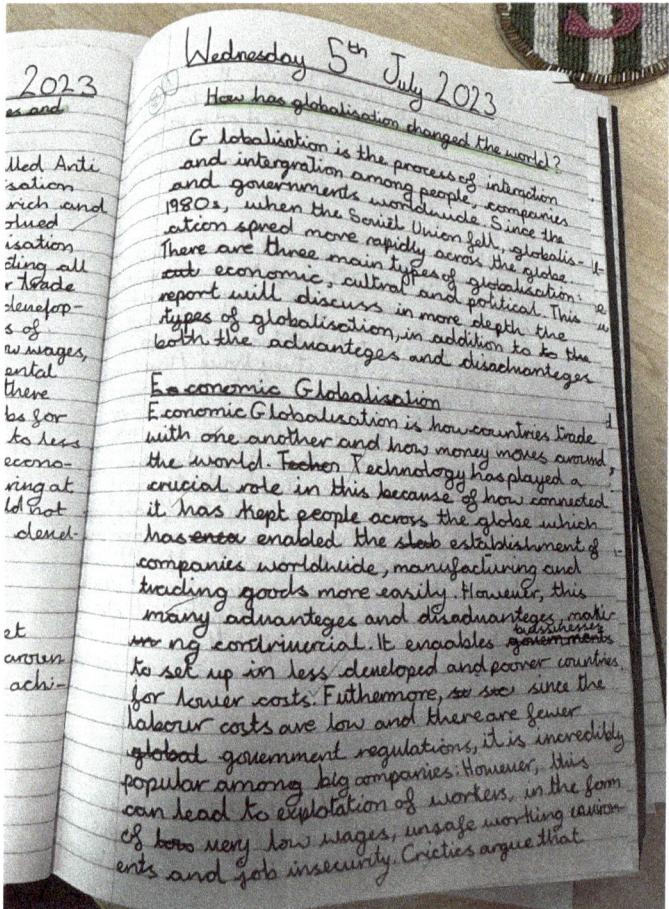

Fig. 3.12 Essay writing in a knowledge-rich curriculum. *source* own photograph

3.7 A Knowledge-Rich Curriculum and Student Achievement

At the supra level, international assessments such as the Programme for International Student Assessment (PISA), organised by the OECD, and Trends in International Mathematics and Science Study (TIMSS), administered by the IEA, are large-scale surveys designed to assess pupil achievement across a number of countries. Some results at these levels seem to indicate that structured knowledge-led approaches lead to better results than skills or competence-based approaches, including for developing applied skills (Crato, 2021, p. 19). Some countries' experiences also point into the same direction. In Portugal, for instance, a structured and knowledge-led curriculum at the macro level led to impressive improvements, followed by a significant drop when this trend was subsequently reversed (Crato, 2022, p. 54–55), both in terms of average student scores and in terms of equal educational opportunities. Although these macro-level statistics are correlational in nature, and can therefore only suggest relations and not determine causal effects, and while we know that the implementation from a written curriculum at the macro level until its enactment in the classroom is quite complex and challenging (Stein et al., 2007), promising experimental evidence at the meso and microlevel seems to corroborate these positive findings with regard to student achievement.

Until recently, the effects of building background knowledge through a knowledge-rich curriculum on primary students' achievement had only been investigated in a limited number of experimentally designed interventions. Those interventions typically focused on building domain and topic knowledge in first, second, and/or third grade with a view to improving reading comprehension, ranged between 1 and 3 years, and showed significant but small, or no effects on standard measures of reading comprehension (Connor et al, 2013; Kim et al., 2021, 2023; See et al., 2015).

However, a recent large-scale experimental study (Grissmer et al., 2023) suggests that the former interventions might not have been implemented early and long enough for larger effects to accumulate. This study measured the long-term effects on Reading/English Language Arts, Science, and Mathematics achievement after 4–7 years of intervention in 14 Charter schools using the Core Knowledge Sequence, which specifies topics and their sequence and suggests materials (Core Knowledge Foundation, 2010). Interestingly, the K-8 curriculum that was used was implemented from kindergarten onwards, and the Reading/ English Language Arts and Mathematics measurements (state achievement data) were collected in 3rd to 6th grade, and those for science in 5th grade. Across all schools, students' Reading/English Language Arts results significantly improved with 16 percentile points, the equivalent of raising US performance from 15th out of 50 countries to the top 5 in the 2016 PIRLS test.

Moreover, as reading and verbal comprehension are essential for further learning in all subjects, these results suggest that students' future achievement is likely to also increase in many other areas. More promising even with a view to educational equality, is the fact that at a low-income school in the sample, achievement gaps at third to sixth grade in Reading/English Language Arts, Science, and Mathematics were completely eliminated, suggesting that systematically building general knowledge in primary school could also help address educational inequality and diminish the Matthew effect (Kaefer et al., 2015; Pfost et al., 2014; Rigney, 2010; Stanovich, 1986). Replicating and extending this study by profoundly analysing knowledge-rich curriculum implementation and enactment, and mapping the intermediating factors and their effects on student achievement may be one of the most crucial endeavours in current educational research.

References

Ausubel, D. P. (1968). *Educational Psychology. A cognitive view*. New York, NY: Holt, Rinehart and Winston, Inc.

Bauersfeld, H. (1979). Research related to the mathematical learning process. In International commission on mathematical instruction (Ed.), *New trends in mathematics teaching* (vol. 4, pp. 199–213). Paris, France: UNESCO.

Britz, J. (1993). *Problem Solving in Early Childhood Classrooms*. ERIC Digest.

Bruner, J. S. (1960). *The process of education*. Harvard University Press.

Connor, C. M., Morrison, F. J., Fishman, B., Crowe, E. C., Al Otaiba, S., & Schatschneider, C. (2013). A longitudinal cluster-randomized controlled study on the accumulating effects of individualized literacy instruction on students' reading from first through third grade. *Psychological Science, 24*(8), 1408–1419.

Core knowledge foundation. (2010). The Core knowledge sequence, ISBN 978-1-890517-25-0, Charlottesville, VA 22902

Crato, N. (2021). *Improving a Country's Education: PISA 2018 Results in 10 Countries*. Springer Nature.

Crato, N. (2025). *Aprender*. Lisbon: FFMS, forthcoming (in Portuguese).

Crato, N. (2022). Math curriculum matters. *European Mathematical Society Magazine, 124*, 49–56.

Cuban, L. (1992). Curriculum stability and change. In P. Jackson (Ed.), *Handbook of research on curriculum* (pp. 216–247). Macmillan.

Deng, Z. (2017). Rethinking curriculum and teaching. *Oxford Research Encyclopedia of Education*.

Dockx, J., Bellens, K., & De Fraine, B. (2020). Do textbooks matter for reading comprehension? A study in Flemish primary education. *Frontiers in Psychology, 10*, 2959.

Eisner, E. W. (1985). *The educational imagination: On the design and evaluation of school programs* (2nd ed.). New York, NY: Macmillan.

Geary, D. C. (2012). Evolutionary educational psychology. In K. R. Harris, S. Graham, T. Urdan, C. B. McCormick, G. M. Sinatra, & J. Sweller (Eds.), *APA educational psychology handbook*, Vol. 1. Theories, constructs, and critical issues (pp. 597–621). American Psychological Association.

Grissmer, D., Buddin, R., Berends, M., Willingham, D., DeCoster, J., Duran, C., Hulleman, C., Murrah, W., & Evans, T. (2023). A kindergarten lottery evaluation of core knowledge charter schools: Should building general knowledge have a central role in educational and social science research and policy? (EdWorkingPaper: 23–755). Retrieved from Annenberg Institute at Brown University.

Hattie, J. (2023). *Visible learning: The sequel: A synthesis of over 2,100 meta-analyses relating to achievement*. Taylor & Francis.

Hirsch, E. D. (2016). *Why knowledge matters: Rescuing our children from failed educational theories*. Harvard Education Press.

Kaefer, T., Neuman, S. B., & Pinkham, A. M. (2015). Pre-existing background knowledge influences socioeconomic differences in preschoolers' word learning and comprehension. *Reading Psychology, 36*(3), 203–231.

Kelly, A. V. (2009). *The curriculum: Theory and Practice*. SAGE Publications.

Kerr, J. F. (Ed.). (1968). *Changing the curriculum*. London, UK: University of London Press.

Kim, J. S., Burkhauser, M. A., Mesite, L. M., Asher, C. A., Relyea, J. E., Fitzgerald, J., & Elmore, J. (2021). Improving reading comprehension, science domain knowledge, and reading engagement through a first-grade content literacy intervention. *Journal of Educational Psychology, 113*(1), 3–26.

Kim, J. S., Burkhauser, M. A., Relyea, J. E., Gilbert, J. B., Scherer, E., Fitzgerald, J., Mosher, D., & McIntyre, J. (2023). A longitudinal randomized trial of a sustained content literacy intervention from first to second grade: Transfer effects on students' reading comprehension. *Journal of Educational Psychology, 115*(1), 73–98.

Kirschner, P. A., & Hendrick, C. (2020). Cognitive Apprenticeship Revisited. *American Educator, 44*(3), 37.

Kirschner, P. A., Hendrick, C., & Heal, J. (2022). *How teaching happens: Seminal works in teaching and teacher effectiveness and what they mean in practice.* Routledge.

Kuiper, W., & Berkvens, J. (Eds.). (2013). *Balancing curriculum regulation and freedom across Europe.* CIDREE.

McTighe, J. (2000). Meaningful learning for all students. *California Curriculum News Report, 25*(5), 4.

Meyer, H. D., & Benavot, A. (Eds.). (2013). *PISA, power, and policy: The emergence of global educational governance.* Symposium Books Ltd.

Muller, J. (2023). Powerful knowledge, disciplinary knowledge, curriculum knowledge: Educational knowledge in question. *International Research in Geographical and Environmental Education, 32*(1), 20–34.

Neuman, S. B., Kaefer, T., & Pinkham, A. (2014). Building background knowledge. *The Reading Teacher, 68*(2), 145–148.

Nieveen, N., & Kuiper, W. (2021). Integral curriculum review in the Netherlands: In need of dovetail joints. In M. Priestley, D. Alvunger, S. Philippou, & T. Soini (Eds.), *Curriculum making in Europe: Policy and practice within and across diverse contexts* (pp. 125–150). Emerald Publishing Limited.

Oates, T. (2014). Why textbooks count. A policy paper. University of Cambridge.

Oates, T. (2011). Could do better: Using international comparisons to refine the National curriculum in England. *Curriculum Journal, 22*(2), 121–150.

Pfost, M., Hattie, J., Dörfler, T., & Artelt, C. (2014). Individual differences in reading development: A review of 25 years of empirical research on Matthew effects in reading. *Review of Educational Research, 84*(2), 203–244.

Popham, James, W., & Baker, L. E. (1970). *Systematic instruction.* Englewood Cliffs, New Jersey: Prentice-Hall.

Portelli, J. P. (1987). On defining curriculum. *Journal of Curriculum and Supervision, 2*(4), 354–367.

Priestley, M., & Sinnema, C. (2014). Downgraded curriculum? An analysis of knowledge in new curricula in Scotland and New Zealand. In *Creating Curricula: Aims, Knowledge and Control* (pp. 61–86). Routledge.

Priestley, M., Philippou, S., Alvunger, D., & Soini, T. (2021). Curriculum making: A conceptual framing. In M. Priestley, D. Alvunger, S. Philippou, & T. Soini (Eds.), *Curriculum making in Europe: Policy and practice within and across diverse contexts* (pp. 1–28). Emerald Publishing Limited.

Rata, E. (2023). Curriculum design: How to design a knowledge-rich school curriculum using the curriculum design coherence model. https://www.nzinitiative.org.nz/research/education/curriculum-design

Rata, E. (2019). Knowledge-rich teaching: A model of curriculum design coherence. *British Educational Research Journal, 45*(4), 681–697.

Rata, E. (2021a). The curriculum design coherence model in the knowledge-rich school project. *Review of Education, 9*(2), 448–495.

Rata, E. (2021b). Context and implications document for the curriculum design coherence model in the knowledge-rich school project. *Review of Education, 9*(2), 496–499.

Reynolds, D., & Hattan, C. (2024). Baseball, presidents, and state test passages: Considering gendered knowledge in literacy research, curricula, and assessments. *The Reading Teacher, 77*(6), 997–1000.

Rigney, D. (2010). *The Matthew effect: How advantage begets further advantage.* Columbia University Press.

Schmidt, W. H., Mcknight, C., & Raizen, S. (1997). *A splintered vision: An investigation of U.S. science and mathematics Education.* Kluwer.

Schmidt, W. H., Houang, R., & Cogan, L. (2002). A coherent curriculum. *American Education, 26*(10), 1–18.

Schmidt, W. H., & Prawat, R. S. (2006). Curriculum coherence and national control of education: Issue or non-issue? *Journal of Curriculum Studies, 38*(6), 641–658.

See, B. H., Gorard, S., & Siddiqui, N. (2015). Word and world reading: Evaluation report and executive summary. Education Endowment Foundation.

Sinnema, C., & Aitken, G. (2013). Emerging international trends in curriculum. In M. Priestley & G. J. J. Biesta (Eds.), *Reinventing the curriculum: New trends in curriculum policy and practice* (pp. 141–163). Bloomsbury Academic.

Sizer, T. R. (1999). That elusive curriculum. *Peabody Journal of Education, 74*(1), 161–165.

Reading Research Quarterly, 21(4), 360–407. Retrieved from http://www.psychologytoday.com/files/u81/Stanovich__1986_pdf

Stein, M., Remillard, J., & Smith, M. (2007). How curriculum influences student learning. In F. K. Lester (Ed.), *Second handbook of research on mathematics teaching and learning* (pp. 319–369). Information Age.

Steiner, D., Magee, J., Jensen, B., & Button, J. (2018). *What we teach matters: How quality curriculum improves student outcomes.* Learning First, Johns Hopkins Institute for Education Policy.

Taba, H. (1962). *Curriculum development: Theory and practice.* Harcourt Brace and World.

Thijs, A., & Van Den Akker, J. (2009). *Curriculum in development.* Netherlands Institute for Curriculum Development.

Tobias, S., & Duffy, T. M. (2009). *Constructivist instruction: Success or failure?* Routledge.

Tyler, R. W. (1949). *Basic principles of curriculum and instruction.* Chicago: University of Chicago Press.

Van den Akker, J. (2003). Curriculum perspectives: An introduction. In J. van den Akker, W. Kuiper, & U. Hameyer (Eds.), *Curriculum landscapes and trends* (pp. 1–10). Netherlands: Springer.

Watkins, C. L. (1997). *Project follow through: A case study of contingencies influencing instructional practices of the educational establishment.* Cambridge Center for Behavioral Studies.

Whitehead, A. N. (1929). *The aims of education and other essays.* The MacMillan Company.

Wiggins, G., & McTighe, J. (2005). *Understanding by design.* Alexandria: Association for Supervision and Curriculum Development.

Wiliam, D. (2013). *Principled curriculum design.* London, UK: SSAT (The Schools Network) Limited.

Wiliam, D. (2014). Principled assessment design. London, UK: SSAT (The Schools Network) Limited. Retrieved from http://www.tauntonteachingalliance.co.uk/wpcontent/uploads/2016/09/Dylan-Wiliam-Principled-assessmentdesign.pdf

Willingham, D. T. (2008). What is developmentally appropriate practice? *American Educator, 32*(2), 34.

Young, M., & Lambert, D. (2014). *Knowledge and the future school. Curriculum and social justice.* Bloomsbury.

Young, M., & Muller, J. (2010). Three educational scenarios for the future: Lessons from the sociology of knowledge. *European Journal of Education, 45*(1), 11–27.

Chapter 4
Concluding Remarks

Over the course of several decades, the position of knowledge within education has been marked by turbulence and notable fluctuations. However, recent advancements in cognitive psychology, and a shift in sociological and democratic perspectives have created a more favourable environment for a revaluation of the concept of knowledge. Now, it has the opportunity to play a central role within education and curriculum: that of the essential condition for future learning. In cognitive psychology, we observed that existing knowledge schemas in long-term memory support human thought so that we can successfully complete complex thinking tasks, such as problem solving, critical thinking, and deep reading comprehension. From a sociological perspective, we noted how distinct epistemological ideas and societal trends changed the perception of knowledge, and how a new school of thought has emphasised its return and vital role for social justice and equitable opportunities for all. In addition, from a democratic standpoint, knowledge has been found crucial in ensuring that individuals are empowered to contribute meaningfully to both societal and professional debates.

All of the above has implications for the curriculum. While earlier, the curriculum either metaphorically tended to promote knowledge tick box behaviour, or, at the other extreme, tended to rely on almost knowledge-free competency-based concepts, we are now evolving towards a knowledge-guided curriculum that values knowledge in itself, yet also attaches specific skills to particular knowledge domains. Although we know that teaching generic skills has little to no transfer, teaching complex skills, such as problem-solving and critical thinking, should not be abandoned. When carefully built with knowledge as a foundation within a domain, we can achieve both knowledge building and complex thinking by engaging deeply with that knowledge. Van Merriënboer and Kirschner (2017) refer to the teaching of this and the support of its achievement as first- and second-order scaffolding. The first positive effects from longitudinal studies of implementing a knowledge-rich curriculum are promising, and we look forward to further research on creating and implementing a curriculum that is characterised by content-richness, coherence, and clarity.

© The Author(s) 2025
T. Surma et al., *Developing Curriculum for Deep Thinking*,
SpringerBriefs in Education, https://doi.org/10.1007/978-3-031-74661-1_4

This rebirth of knowledge in the curriculum has various implications for the field of education. In some cases, the curriculum has been underplayed in educational policymaking, often focusing on issues such as the structure and governance of education systems or qualification frameworks. While these are important matters, what children and young people learn is of central importance and should therefore lie at the heart of educational policy. An effective system is marked by coherence, in which all aspects of the educational system are well aligned with each other, not only within and across subjects in the form of clear learning progressions, but also in the form of assessment, inspectorate, teacher autonomy, accountability, professional development, etc. Based on the rationale and educational purposes, the curriculum is at the heart of this process. A knowledge-rich curriculum should therefore be designed for coherence and progression using effective design methods. Coherence and progression are created by connecting big ideas, specific content, knowledge and complex skills aiming at full knowledge engagement, a concept-cohering process that connects the curriculum material to students' cognition. Dangers, however, lie in the fact that the curriculum can become a political football field in which government officials and other educational stakeholders constantly add their own favourite elements, including all of the societal problems that education is expected to solve but is not capable of solving, as happened with the secondary English Language curriculum in England. Another risk is problematic consensus-seeking, resulting in vague and unclearly formulated learning goals, affecting both curricular coherence and clarity. Decisions will have to be made. Therefore, an arm-length curriculum body is best tasked with formulating and revising the curriculum. For example, a planned cycle of regular reviews should be incorporated into the curriculum development process and be a statutory task of the curriculum body.

Finally, a knowledge-led curriculum also has implications for teachers' education and professional development. The introduction of a knowledge-rich curriculum needs to be accompanied by an extensive program of continuous professional development (CPD) for teachers and school leaders, and will involve significant changes in the curriculum for initial teacher education. Teacher education and ongoing CPD initiatives should include the principles and methods of effective knowledge design. Teachers should understand how coherence occurs, how subject concepts connect to materialised content, why engagement with knowledge should follow the subject concept-content selection, and the relationship between this concept-cohering curriculum and the intellectual processes which build students' cognitive architecture. Teacher quality remains paramount to successfully implement a knowledge-rich curriculum.

Designing a coherent curriculum is not an easy task and requires thorough thinking. "As a result, curriculum is, and should be, a most contested topic, the essence of democratic debate, and the core debate about what is taught and valued in schools" (Hattie, 2023, p. 304).

References

Hattie, J. (2023). *Visible learning: The sequel: A synthesis of over 2100 meta-analyses relating to achievement*. Taylor & Francis.

Van Merriënboer, J. J., & Kirschner, P. A. (2017). *Ten steps to complex learning: A systematic approach to four-component instructional design*. Routledge.

Chapter 5
Executive Summary

Nearly all teachers and other stakeholders in education pursue a common aim: we want the students whom we teach and guide during their formative years to think deeply about what we teach them. We want them to be able to go beyond their current experiences and have a deep understanding of the world. We want them to be able to think critically, work together, solve problems, read for understanding, and perform many other complex tasks. This book discusses why the apparently obvious strategy of simply teaching children how to think deeply does not work and offers an alternative way forward. It reviews the evidence for the prominent role of knowledge in how we learn, think, read, understand, and solve problems, drawing ideas from cognitive psychology, educational psychology, sociology, and curriculum studies, combined with real-life classroom experiences. Its goal is to elucidate why a knowledge-rich curriculum is not only the soundest way forward to both effectively teach knowledge and complex skills in school, but is also crucial if we hope to achieve equitable opportunities for all students.

5.1 How Knowledge Matters

5.1.1 Knowledge Matters: A Learning Perspective

When we speak of knowledge in educational systems, we refer to biologically secondary knowledge (Geary & Berch, 2016) which, as opposed to biologically primary knowledge, cannot be acquired spontaneously, and must be consciously taught and effortfully learned. Examples include reading and writing, solving algebraic problems, and engaging in discussions about geographical, scientific, political, cultural, and historical phenomena. From a cognitive psychology standpoint, the

© The Author(s) 2025
T. Surma et al., *Developing Curriculum for Deep Thinking*,
SpringerBriefs in Education, https://doi.org/10.1007/978-3-031-74661-1_5

value of a well-established knowledge base for learning is unequivocally recognised. Humans have the capacity to construct a robust knowledge base within long-term memory, which provides us with resources to enhance the efficacy of working memory during cognitive tasks (Baddeley & Andrade, 2000; Baddeley & Hitch, 1974). What you know determines what you see (Kirschner, 1991). The more extensive one's knowledge base is in terms of both its breadth and depth, the more easily new knowledge is acquired and remembered (Alexander et al., 1994; Ausubel, 1968; Shapiro, 2004). Complex schemas of interconnected ideas can then serve as conceptual coat hangers or anchors for the organisation of knowledge and learning new ideas (Hattie, 2023). However, knowledge alone does not lead to improved learning. To be effective, prior knowledge must be activated, relevant, and congruent. Then its impact on learning can be significant (Brod, 2021). Knowledge is also crucial for carrying out complex cognitive skills, such as critical thinking (you think critically about something; Willingham, 2019), problem solving (you solve problems in something; De Bruyckere et al., 2020; Thorndike, 1923; Willingham, 2021), and reading comprehension (you can decode and subsequently comprehend something written about something; Kendeou & Van Den Broek, 2007; Kintsch, 1998; Kintsch & van Dijk, 1978; McCarthy & McNamara, 2021; Willingham, 2017). Indeed, seemingly counterintuitively, the best ways to become proficient in a skill often do not resemble the skill itself (Wiliam, 2018). The more robust one's knowledge base, the more seamlessly and efficiently these complex cognitive skills—precisely, those teachers aim to develop in their students—are acquired and can be carried out.

5.1.2   Knowledge Matters: A Sociological Perspective

Our perspective on knowledge is shaped by the lens through which we view it. When examining knowledge from a sociological perspective, it is evident that its significance has been subject to fluctuating societal trends. Societal viewpoints have, at times, overshadowed the importance of knowledge, yet social realists (Barrett, 2024), sociological theorists who have emerged as successors of constructivist thinkers (Rata, 2024a), agree that focusing on rich and broad content knowledge ensures that all students, regardless of background, have equal access to a foundational body of knowledge, reducing disparities, and promoting a more inclusive educational experience. For this reason, they argue for the need to 'bring knowledge back in' (2024a; Muller, 2000; Rata, 2012; Wheelahan, 2007; Young, 2007). In that regard, Young (2009, 2013) produced a theory of powerful knowledge, acknowledging that while knowledge is socially produced, some types of knowledge are more powerful, and, yes, 'better', than others. He positions the production of powerful knowledge within specific social and intellectual groups, often represented by academic disciplines. This disciplinary knowledge then needs to be translated by expert teachers and subject specialists, thus providing students with more dependable interpretations and insights into the world, and allowing them to think about topics and subjects their experiences alone would have never let them have access to.

5.1.3 Knowledge Matters: A Democratic Perspective

Deciding what our children should learn does not only play a role in what we want the future for our society to be like, but also in who we want our children to become. This leads us to a very difficult question: What kind of knowledge is that important that we will not leave its transmission up to chance? A question that becomes even more difficult to answer as the production of knowledge in our society grows. One could argue that the response to this question depends heavily on the answer to an other question: What is the purpose of education? Although there are many possible answers, most can be divided into four broad categories: personal empowerment, cultural transmission, preparation for work, and preparation for citizenship (Wiliam, 2013). These broad philosophies do not exclude one another, but are sometimes in conflict. A balance is needed, as one without the other can have unwanted consequences. When examining knowledge from a democratic perspective, one cannot overlook the ideas of E.D. Hirsch and his notions of cultural literacy, which he defined as "possessing the basic information needed to thrive in the modern world" (Hirsch, 1988, p. XIII). When communicating, we assume a vast amount of shared background knowledge. For disadvantaged students, who may face limitations in exposure to a rich array of experiences and information outside schools, this can limit them, not due to a lack of ability, but because of a lack of access to knowledge. This is why, when knowledge is no longer explicitly addressed in schools, or assumed to be primarily constructed from children's own experiences, the most disadvantaged students suffer the most. This is problematic not only for these individuals but also for society as a whole. As Hirsch (2009) states, shared knowledge fosters a sense of commonality among diverse citizens in a democratic society. In a society characterised by cultural diversity, a common body of knowledge ensures that citizens can engage in informed discussions, debates, and decision-making processes. It promotes a sense of belonging and inclusivity as individuals draw upon shared references that go beyond individual differences. When access to this shared knowledge is hindered or not evenly distributed, issues of inequality in education may widen. This is why the erosion of the role of knowledge within the educational landscape can have dire consequences (Hirsch, 2016).

Social realists (Barrett, 2024) share Hirsch's views on the importance of knowledge in our society and its vital role in education. Yet, they relocate (powerful) knowledge within academic disciplines, making what is taught and learned in classrooms more reflective of the characteristics of disciplinary knowledge developed by specialist communities. They also share Hirsch's view on knowledge as a prerequisite for fostering equitable opportunities for all and social justice. Wheelahan (2010) further strengthens this viewpoint from a democratic perspective, emphasising the crucial role of disciplinary knowledge as socially powerful knowledge. It arms students with the language to participate in discussions on politics, morality, environmentalism, migration, and many other topics prevalent in civil society. Furthermore, it also gives them the capacity to scrutinise the foundations of knowledge, the authority upon which it stands, and thus, the tools to be critical of it (Young,

2007). In sum, while deciding what knowledge ought to be provided to our children will (and should!) always be the result of societal debate, ensuring that knowledge itself is not forgotten is crucial for equitable opportunities for all and our democratic society. Hirsch has shown the importance of a common knowledge base and helped bring knowledge back into conversation, whereas social realism has brought knowledge back into social theory, while at the same time emphasising the importance of the disciplinary aspect of knowledge. All these factors have implications for the curriculum.

5.2 Knowledge and the Curriculum

5.2.1 Everything Starts with the Curriculum

The curriculum is complex in its conceptualisation and how it is made and takes form in our educational institutions. For the sake of clarity and for the purpose of this book, we define the curriculum as a 'plan for learning over time' (Taba, 1962; Thijs & van den Akker, 2009). Highlighting some factors regarding the complexity of curriculum as a concept may help clarify why curriculum is at the centre of so many educational debates, and why these debates are so important. A first factor to consider is the broad or narrow perspective that you adopt when considering the concept of 'curriculum'. Learning is not limited to what happens at school; students' social environment also plays a significant role. These aspects are also referred to as the societal curriculum (Deng, 2017). In this book we focus on the content and learning activities organised at school and the system behind it (Tyler, 1949; Popham & Baker, 1970), yet we take into consideration these important factors that can influence the learning potential of students.

A second, and perhaps even more important, factor is the fact that the curriculum depends on a conception of education and learning. What do we value as society, as schools, as teachers, and what is the goal of schooling? The work of Tyler (1949) and van den Akker (2003) provides us with valuable guidelines in this regard. A third factor to consider is that determining what we want students to learn does not automatically equal what students actually learn, due to discrepancies between the intended curriculum (what we want students to learn), the implemented curriculum (how these intended learning goals are then enacted), and the attained curriculum (what students actually learned) (van den Akker, 2009). Besides the curricular intentions, teachers and textbooks also act as mediating factors in what is actually taught to students. Due to the way in which the school's work is planned and organised, and through the materials provided students can also learn things that are not overtly included in the curriculum, the so-called hidden curriculum (Kelly, 2009). All of the above then leads to a fourth factor, namely that the curriculum can be organised at different levels, which Priestley and colleagues (2021) categorise as (1) the supra level; (2) the macro level; (3) the meso level; (4) the micro level; and (5) the nano level. In sum, considering the context and rationale at the different levels, and taking into account the insights about the intended, implemented, attained, and hidden curriculum, it can easily be concluded that implementing a curriculum is indeed complex and should be subject to thorough debate.

5.2.2 Curriculum as a Pendulum

Over the years the role of knowledge in the curriculum has, like a pendulum, shifted between two extremes, from highly visible to virtually invisible knowledge elements. These extremes can be positioned in Young and Muller's (2010) perspectives of thinking about curriculum, which they labelled 'futures'. The former, with highly visible knowledge elements, corresponds with the so called Future 1, where a curriculum can be described as a collection of learning content, treating knowledge as fixed, unchanging, and based on tradition. The latter, with virtually invisible knowledge elements, corresponds with Future 2 and prioritises an outcome-based curriculum that reduces knowledge's central role in further learning and in developing complex skills. It is important to underline that the historical shift from Future 1 to Future 2-curriculum involved the elimination of both the negative ánd the positive elements of Future 1, which is why a curricular return to knowledge must consider the lessons learned from both futures (Muller, 2023). Social realists have termed this solution Future 3, from here on referred to as a 'knowledge-rich curriculum'.

5.2.3 Towards the Best of Both Worlds: A Knowledge-Rich Curriculum

A knowledge-rich curriculum constitutes a plan for learning over time that is concept-led and knowledge-led (Oates, 2011), which encompasses a wide range of specified knowledge, and provides ample depth and opportunities to engage with that knowledge (Rata, 2021). It sets high expectations for all students and systematically builds their knowledge of words and the world (Hirsch, 2016). It aims at a broad and steady foundation for complex thinking skills, such as critical thinking and reading comprehension, as well as knowledge building, which are further amplified and deepened by these complex skills. A comprehensive knowledge-rich curriculum covers subjects and concepts that go beyond children's day-to-day experiences and is based on the 'best' disciplinary knowledge available at that time (Young & Lambert, 2014). It ensures that every child has access to a broad and solid knowledge base in school, even if it has not been (partially) acquired from an early age onwards outside school. Three overarching principles were found to be most beneficial for understanding how a knowledge-rich curriculum can enhance learning: (1) content richness, (2) coherence, and (3) clarity.

In terms of content richness, four important elements are thoroughly discussed: (a) which content to select; (b) on what basis choices can be made; (c) how hierarchy and structure in knowledge have an impact on sequence; and (d) how to balance knowledge and skills in a knowledge-rich curriculum. Curriculum coherence entails (a) vertical coherence, that is, considering the organisation of the concepts and content within it, which is vital if one is to create a seamless and logical conceptual progression in what students learn over time; and (b) horizontal coherence, that is, how these concepts align with each other across subjects (Thijs & van den Akker, 2009). Moreover, it should also consider (c) the structure of the knowledge itself (Schmidt et al., 2002; Rata, 2021). Big ideas can be used as a starting point, which can subsequently be broken down into several important components, such as what needs to be assessed, what evidence is needed to determine whether students really understand certain concepts, and what students need to be able to know and do (Hattie, 2023; McTighe, 2000; Wiggins & McTighe, 2005; William, 2013). Clarity is the third important feature of a knowledge-rich curriculum. In view of setting clear expectations, the following elements are discussed: (a) emphasising the importance of clear goals for teachers and student learning; (b) interpreting learning objectives and their impact on the discrepancy between the intended and the achieved curriculum; and (c) the importance of good alignment in the educational system.

5.2.4 A Knowledge-Rich Curriculum and Student Achievement

Until recently, the effects of building background knowledge through a knowledge-rich curriculum on primary students' achievement had only been investigated in a limited number of experimentally designed interventions, and showed small, or no effects on student achievement (Conor et al., 2013, Kim, et al., 2021; Kim et al., 2023; See et al., 2015). However, a recent large-scale experimental study (Grissmer et al., 2023) suggests that the former interventions might not have been implemented early or long enough for larger effects to accumulate. The K-8 Core Knowledge Sequence was implemented In 14 U.S. Charter schools from kindergarten onwards, and after four to seven years of intervention across all schools, students' Reading/English Language Arts results significantly improved with 16 percentile points, the equivalent of raising US performance from 15th out of 50 countries to the top five in the 2016 PIRLS test. A low-income school in the sample showed even more promising results, completely eliminating achievement gaps at third to sixth grade in Reading/English Language Arts, Science, and Mathematics. This suggests that systematically building background knowledge in primary school could also help address educational inequality and diminish the Matthew effect (Rigney, 2010; Stanovich, 1986). Replicating and extending this study may be one of the most crucial endeavours in current educational research.

5.3 Concluding Remarks

Revitalised by contemporary democratic and social perspectives, and bolstered by consistent findings from cognitive psychology, we are now witnessing a revival of the importance of knowledge in education. It has now re-emerged as a prerequisite for improved learning, critical thinking, problem-solving and reading comprehension, as a facilitator for collective discourse, and as a catalyst for equitable opportunities for all. All of the above has implications for the curriculum. Earlier, the curriculum either tended to promote knowledge tick box behaviour, or, on the other extreme, tended to rely on almost knowledge-free competency-based concepts. We are now evolving towards a knowledge-guided curriculum that values knowledge in itself, yet also attaches specific skills to particular knowledge domains. Although we know that teaching generic skills has little to no transfer, teaching complex skills, such as problem-solving and critical thinking, should not be abandoned. When carefully built with knowledge as a foundation within a domain, we can achieve both knowledge building and complex thinking by engaging deeply with that knowledge. The first positive effects from longitudinal studies of implementing a knowledge-rich curriculum are promising, and we look forward to further research on creating and implementing a curriculum that is characterised by content richness, coherence, and clarity.

References

Alexander, P., Kulikowich, J., & Schulze, S. (1994). How subject-matter knowledge affects recall and interest. *American Educational Research Journal, 31*(2), 313–337.

Ausubel, D.P. (1968). *Educational Psychology. A cognitive view.* New York, NY: Holt, Rinehart and Winston, Inc.

Baddeley, A., & Hitch, G. (1974). Working memory. In G. H. Bower (Ed.), *The Psychology of Learning and Motivation: Advances in Research and Theory* vol. 8, pp. 47–89. Academic Press.

Baddeley, A. D., & Andrade, J. (2000). Working memory and the vividness of imagery. *Journal of Experimental Psychology: General, 129*, 126–145.

Barrett, B. (2024). 'Rob Moore, Social Realism, and the Sociology of Education and Knowledge', in Rata, E. (Ed.), *Research Handbook in Curriculum and Education.* Edward Elgar Publishing. Chapter 5, pp. 79–87.

Brod, G. (2021). Toward an understanding of when prior knowledge helps or hinders learning. *npj Science of Learning, 6*(1), 24.

Connor, C. M., Morrison, F. J., Fishman, B., Crowe, E. C., Al Otaiba, S., & Schatschneider, C. (2013). A longitudinal cluster-randomized controlled study on the accumulating effects of individualized literacy instruction on students' reading from first through third grade. *Psychological Science, 24*(8), 1408–1419.

De Bruyckere, P., Kirschner, P. A., & Hulshof, C. D. (2020). If you learn A, will you be better able to learn B? Understanding transfer of learning. *American Educator, 44*, 30–34.

Deng, Z. (2017). Rethinking curriculum and teaching. *Oxford Research Encyclopedia of Education.*

Geary, D., & Berch, D. (2016). Evolution and children's cognitive and academic development. In D. Geary & D. Berch (Eds.), *Evolutionary perspectives on child development and education* (pp. 217–249). Springer.

Grissmer, D., Buddin, R., Berends, M., Willingham, D., DeCoster, J., Duran, C., Hulleman, C., Murrah, W., & Evans, T. (2023). A kindergarten lottery evaluation of core knowledge charter schools: Should building general knowledge have a central role in educational and social science research and policy? (EdWorkingPaper: 23-755). Retrieved from Annenberg Institute at Brown University.

Hattie, J. (2023). *Visible learning: The sequel: A synthesis of over 2,100 meta-analyses relating to achievement*. Taylor & Francis.

Hirsch, E. D. (1988). *Cultural literacy: What every American needs to know*. Vintage.

Hirsch, E. D. (2009). *The making of Americans: Democracy and our schools*. Yale University Press.

Hirsch, E. D. (2016). *Why knowledge matters: Rescuing our children from failed educational theories*. Harvard Education Press.

Kelly, A. V. (2009). *The curriculum: Theory and Practice*. SAGE Publications.

Kendeou, P., & Van Den Broek, P. (2007). The effects of prior knowledge and text structure on comprehension processes during reading of scientific texts. *Memory and Cognition, 35*(7), 1567–1577.

Kim, J. S., Burkhauser, M. A., Mesite, L. M., Asher, C. A., Relyea, J. E., Fitzgerald, J., & Elmore, J. (2021). Improving reading comprehension, science domain knowledge, and reading engagement through a first-grade content literacy intervention. *Journal of Educational Psychology, 113*(1), 3–26.

Kim, J. S., Burkhauser, M. A., Relyea, J. E., Gilbert, J. B., Scherer, E., Fitzgerald, J., Mosher, D., & McIntyre, J. (2023). A longitudinal randomized trial of a sustained content literacy intervention from first to second grade: Transfer effects on students' reading comprehension. *Journal of Educational Psychology, 115*(1), 73–98.

Kintsch, W. (1998). *Comprehension: A paradigm for cognition*. Cambridge University Press.

Kintsch, W., & van Dijk, T. A. (1978). Toward a model of text comprehension and production. *Psychological Review, 85*(5), 363–394.

Kirschner, P. A. (1991). *Practicals in higher science education*. [Doctoral Thesis, Open Universiteit: faculties and services]. Open Universiteit.

McCarthy, K. S., & McNamara, D. S. (2021). The multidimensional knowledge in text comprehension framework. *Educational Psychologist., 56*(3), 196–214.

McTighe, J. (2000). Meaningful learning for all students. *California Curriculum News Report, 25*(5), 4.

Muller, J. (2000). *Reclaiming knowledge. Social theory, curriculum and education policy*. Routledge.

Muller, J. (2023). Powerful knowledge, disciplinary knowledge, curriculum knowledge: Educational knowledge in question. *International Research in Geographical and Environmental Education, 32*(1), 20–34.

Oates, T. (2011). Could do better: Using international comparisons to refine the National Curriculum In England. *Curriculum Journal, 22*(2), 121–150.

Popham, James, W. & Baker, L.E. (1970). *Systematic instruction*. Englewood Cliffs, New Jersey: Prentice-Hall.

Priestley, M., Philippou, S., Alvunger, D., & Soini, T. (2021). Curriculum making: A conceptual framing. In M. Priestley, D. Alvunger, S. Philippou, & T. Soini (Eds.), *Curriculum making in Europe: Policy and practice within and across diverse contexts* (pp. 1–28). Emerald Publishing Limited.

Rata, E. (2012). The politics of knowledge in education. *British Educational Research Journal, 38*, 103–124.

Rata, E. (2024). Introduction: social realism, didaktik, and cognitive science in curriculum and education. In E. Rata (Ed.), *Research Handbook on Curriculum and Education* (pp. 1–18). Edward Elgar Publishing.

Rigney, D. (2010). *The Matthew effect: How advantage begets further advantage*. Columbia University Press.

Schmidt, W. H., Houang, R., & Cogan, L. (2002). A coherent curriculum. *American Education, 26*(10), 1–18.

See, B. H., Gorard, S., & Siddiqui, N. (2015). Word and world reading: Evaluation report and executive Summary. Education Endowment Foundation.

Shapiro, A. (2004). How including prior knowledge as a subject variable may change outcomes of learning research. *American Educational Research Journal, 41*(1), 159–189.

Stanovich, K. E. (1986). Matthew effects in reading: Some consequences of individual differences in the acquisition of literacy. *Reading Research Quarterly, 21*(4), 360-407. Retrieved from http://www.psychologytoday.com/files/u81/Stanovich__1986_.pdf

Taba, H. (1962). *Curriculum development: Theory and practice*. Harcourt Brace and World.

Thijs, A., & Van Den Akker, J. (2009). *Curriculum in development*. Netherlands Institute for Curriculum Development.

Thorndike, E. L. (1923). The infuence of first-year Latin upon ability to read English. *School and Society, 17*, 165–168.

Tyler, R. W. (1949). *Basic principles of curriculum and instruction*. Chicago: University of Chicago Press.

Van den Akker, J. (2003). Curriculum perspectives: An introduction. In J. van den Akker, W. Kuiper, & U. Hameyer (Eds.), *Curriculum Landscapes and Trends* (pp. 1–10). Springer.

Wheelahan, L. (2010). *Why knowledge matters in curriculum: A social realist argument*. Routledge.

Wheelahan, L. (2007). How competency-based training locks the working class out of powerful knowledge: A modified Bernsteinian analysis. *British Journal of Sociology of Education, 28*(5), 637–651.

Wiggins, G., & McTighe, J. (2005). *Understanding by design*. Alexandria: Association for Supervision and Curriculum Development.

Wiliam, D. (2013). *Principled curriculum design*. London, UK: SSAT (The Schools Network) Limited.

Wiliam, D. (2018). *Creating the schools our children need*. Learning Sciences International.

Willingham, D.T. (2019). How to teach critical thinking. NSW Department of Education. Retrieved from https://education.nsw.gov.au/teaching-and-learning/education-for-a-changing-world/resource-library/how-to-teach-critical-thinking.html

Willingham, D.T. (2021). *Why don't students like school? A cognitive scientist answers questions about how the mind works and what it means for the classroom*. John Wiley & Sons.

Willingham, D. T. (2017). *The reading mind. A cognitive approach to understanding how the mind reads*. Jossey-Bass.

Young, M. (2007). *Bringing knowledge back in: From social constructivism to social realism in the sociology of education*. Routledge.

Young, M., & Lambert, D. (2014). *Knowledge and the future school. Curriculum and social justice*. Bloomsbury.

Young, M. (2009). Education, globalisation and the voice of knowledge. *Journal of Education and Work, 22*(3), 193–204.

Young, M. (2013). Overcoming the crisis in curriculum theory: A knowledge-based approach. *Journal of Curriculum Studies, 45*(2), 101–108.

Young, M., & Muller, J. (2010). Three educational scenarios for the future: Lessons from the sociology of knowledge. *European Journal of Education, 45*(1), 11–27.

Appendix
How is Knowledge Remembered?

Let's explore what it takes to store knowledge effectively in our long-term memory.

As stated earlier, a key element in learning is what we already know. It's much easier to add new information to an organised set of existing knowledge than to start learning something completely new. However, when we don't have much relevant prior knowledge, we face the challenge of our working memory's limited capacity and need to find ways to efficiently process all the new information coming in.

There are two main challenges with long-term memory: first, developing effective ways to encode information so that it's fully processed and second, using retrieval strategies that make it easier to access memories. There's a wealth of books and articles on learning principles that address both challenges, which are valuable resources for further reading. To give you a starting point, we will outline some key learning strategies that relate to learning and teaching the curriculum (Table A.1).

Based on Winne & Nesbit, 2010; Dunlosky et al., 2013; Hattie & Yates, 2013; Koedinger et al., 2013

© The Editor(s) (if applicable) and The Author(s) 2025
T. Surma et al., *Developing Curriculum for Deep Thinking*,
SpringerBriefs in Education, https://doi.org/10.1007/978-3-031-74661-1

Table A.1 principles that promote durable learning

Learning principle	Learners benefit when …
Worked examples	They see how success looks like instead of being left to discovery methods. Worked examples provide a form of modelling through demonstrations of successful procedures or products.
Dual code and multimedia	Words are accompanied by relevant pictures. Our working memory can combine words and images efficiently.
Coherence	Materials and multimedia explicitly link related concepts to each other and minimise distracting irrelevant material.
Segmentation	Complex new information is broken down into manageable and structured subparts.
Prior knowledge	Relevant prior knowledge is activated.
Multiple examples	Multiple examples (such as concrete and varied representations, stories) are provided, compared.
Practice	New knowledge is practiced.
Interest	Content is grounded in real-world issues that hold significance for the learner.
Spaced practice	Learning sessions are spaced over time compared to massing learning sessions.
Retrieval practice	They retrieve information from memory compared to recognise or reread information.
Generative practice	They think about and produce explanations, outlines, summaries, drawings, answers, mindmaps from memory compared to having them recognise or reread information.
Scaffolding	Support is adjusted to learners needs, and removed when they get more knowledgeable.
Interleaved practice	Practice sessions intermix different comparable knowledge and skills compared to practicing them in a block fashion.
Test expectation	They expect a final test or exam.
Feedback	Feedback on their performance in a learning task is provided.
Questioning and explaining	They pose and answer deep-level questions that elicit explanations.
Self-regulated learning	They receive explicit instruction in how to self-regulate their learning as learners often lack an an accurate understanding of their own cognitive processes.

References

Uncited References

Dunlosky, J., Rawson, K. A., Marsh, E. J., Nathan, M. J., & Willingham, D. T. (2013). Improving students' learning with effective learning techniques: Promising directions from cognitive and educational psychology. *Psychological Science in the Public Interest, 14*(1), 4–58.

Hattie, J., & Yates, G. C. (2013). *Visible learning and the science of how we learn.* Routledge.

Koedinger, K. R., Booth, J. L., & Klahr, D. (2013). Instructional complexity and the science to constrain it. *Science, 342*(6161), 935–937.

Winne, P. H., & Nesbit, J. C. (2010). The psychology of academic achievement. *Annual Review of Psychology, 61*(1), 653–678.

www.ingramcontent.com/pod-product-compliance
Lightning Source LLC
Chambersburg PA
CBHW050218220125
20610CB00009B/70